DATE DUE

MR 31 '98			
AP 2 '98			
JY 30 '98			

DEMCO 38-296

Contemporary Portraits of Japanese Women

/2

Contemporary Portraits of Japanese Women

YUKIKO TANAKA

PRAEGER

Westport, Connecticut
London

Library of Congress Cataloging-in-Publication Data

Tanaka, Yukiko.
Contemporary portraits of Japanese women / Yukiko Tanaka.
p. cm.
Includes bibliographical references and index.
ISBN 0–275–95067–0 (alk. paper) . —ISBN 0–275–95173–1
(pbk. : alk. paper)
1. Women—Japan—Social conditions. I. Title.
HQ1762.T339   1995
305.42′0952—dc20   94–39944

British Library Cataloguing in Publication Data is available.

Library of Congress Catalog Card Number: 94–39944
ISBN: 0–275–95067–0
0–275–95173–1 (pbk.)

First published in 1995

Praeger Publishers, 88 Post Road West, Westport, CT 06881
An imprint of Greenwood Publishing Group, Inc.

Printed in the United States of America

The paper used in this book complies with the
Permanent Paper Standard issued by the National
Information Standards Organization (Z39.48–1984).

10 9 8 7 6 5 4 3 2 1

Contents

Introduction

This book is not intended to present an all-inclusive treatment of women in contemporary Japan. Instead I have tried to present to the Western reader a collage of subjects and issues that seem especially relevant to me, either because of my personal experience (or the experiences of friends and acquaintances in Japan) or because the subjects clearly command the attention of Japanese women and are interesting in light of comparable issues in other countries. My voice is basically that of a critic, a woman who grew up in Japan from 1940 to 1969 but eventually established some distance from her country. Behind the bright picture of economic figures and portfolios that dominated Western media reporting on the "Land of the Rising Sun" were shadows, in the form of problems resulting from dramatic changes in lifestyle, particularly for women and children. This book will show some of these problems, as well as favorable changes; it will present realities being lived by Japanese women today, in marriage and family life, motherhood and child rearing, work and social participation. The tableau that emerges will depict a more complete picture of Japan today.

The changes that have occurred in Japan in my lifetime have been immense indeed. To begin with, from 1954 till 1973, when the dramatic worldwide increase in the price of crude oil took place, the Japanese economy grew at an unprecedented rate of 10 percent per year. This was three times greater than the average annual growth before World War II, and twice the American and European annual growth rates during the same period. The visual landscape of Japan was changing rapidly. For example, while in 1950 only 2 percent of Japanese roads were paved, by 1975, 34 percent were; in 1945, urban dwellers represented only 28 percent of the entire population, but, by 1970, the figure had mushroomed to 72 percent (in the United States, the increase was from 64 to 73.5 percent between 1950 and 1970).[1] In 1962, Tokyo became the largest city in the world, with a population approaching 10 million.

The shift from being an agricultural to an industrial nation began in Japan as late as the 1950s, but the transition was completed considerably more quickly than in Western nations. By the beginning of the 1970s, Japan boasted highly developed manufacturing and service industries. The economy was fueled by a diligent, well-educated, and poorly paid work force. This generation of workers had been born between the world wars and had experienced hardship in its youth. Husbands worked longer hours, leaving all the household chores and child rearing to their wives; such men earned the nickname of "corporate soldiers."[2] Gender-role division among married couples, already clearly defined, became even more rigid during this period. Behind workers' willingness to accept low wages and a corporate policy of reinvesting profits was also a national drive to catch up with Western industrial powers.

As a result of this high economic growth, household income went up. Between 1965 and 1973, for example, it rose an average (after inflation) of 5.8 percent a year. The standard of living improved, and the Japanese lifestyle became more Westernized; people ate more meat and dairy products and less rice. This was the period that showed the beginnings of conspicuous consumption. The number of automobiles purchased increased fifteen-fold between 1960 and 1980. Mass production and a more efficient distribution system lowered the cost of home appliances, creating more free time and enabling housewives to work at part-time jobs. The modern nuclear family was slowly replacing the three-generational household.

In the 1960s, the Japanese lived in the "present tense," paying little attention to the possible ramifications of rapid economic growth and the resulting changes in social and personal life. The 1970s were a more sobering decade, when people began to see the unpleasant side of unbridled development: industrial pollution, soaring land prices, overcrowded living conditions, and a dangerous dependency on foreign natural resources, especially oil. Consumer prices rose sharply in the mid-1970s. Couples began to have fewer children because of the high cost of housing and education; the average life expectancy steadily rose, resulting in a sharp increase in the numbers of elderly.

Still, these seemed minor setbacks for a country that continued to enjoy economic success and increasing world attention during the 1980s. And some positive changes were occurring in the social arena. Women made progress in the workplace, winning sex discrimination cases and obtaining opportunities to work as seriously as men and to be promoted accordingly. This trend partly reflects the fact that more women worked longer years instead of quitting work at marriage. The 1980s were heralded by the Japanese media as "The Age of Women." A few women were able to play an influential political role, as women in general became more interested in making their voices heard on important social issues. The visit of Hillary Rodham Clinton in the summer of 1993 touched off great excitement among younger Japanese women—some of whom believe that they can pursue ways of life that women of my generation, not to mention my mother's generation, could not foresee.

For those watching from the outside, particularly for American feminists, conditions for women in Japan may still seem remarkably backward in many ways. Because of the high value that Japanese society places upon tradition, change there comes slowly and unevenly. The contributions that women have made to their nation's economic miracle—by playing roles both traditional and nontraditional (and paying the price for it)—have not been small. In my opinion, their contribution has not been properly valued in Japan as it has been elsewhere.

I was born near the city of Yokohama, now a part of the Tōkai megalopolis, an industrial region that stretches for a few hundred miles, from the northern edge of metropolitan Tokyo almost to the foot of Mount Fuji. Until a decade after the end of World War II, the neighborhood where I grew up was essentially a farming community. All of its land is now used to accommodate houses, shops, paved roads, and parking spaces.

The first five years of my life belong to the war years; my memory retains the sound of bombing aircraft that shattered window panes and shrieking sirens telling us to evacuate to a shelter. Sometimes we stayed for a long time in our shelter, a natural cave in a nearby hill that was shared by all of our neighbors. Rather than being scared and miserable, I enjoyed these occasions, which were almost pleasant social gatherings. My mother has subsequently recounted how brave I was in walking many miles and staying with strangers in a mountainous village where I was sent later as the war progressed.

When I reflect on the postwar years, the first picture that comes to mind is of a long line of people holding bowls in their hands in front of a market. To help my mother, I sometimes stood in line with the rest to buy fish and other essential foods that were being rationed—rice, soy sauce, and salt. Most people who lived in the cities did not have quite enough to eat; those who had money relied on the black market, but others remained hungry. I do not recall being hungry, but that was because my mother exchanged some of her kimonos with local farmers for food. We grew a few vegetables in our small yard. All of our neighbors spent a great deal of time and energy helping each other get enough to eat. Even when conditions improved years later, the habit of sharing and exchanging food persisted among our friends and neighbors.

Housing was also scarce after the war, and so people shared houses as well. My mother's younger sister and her husband and baby lived with the four of us—my parents, my younger brother, and myself—in our three-bedroom house for several years until they managed to find a place of their own. My maternal grandparents lived with us on and off, too; they had lost both their house and their lumber business during the war. Although it was traditional for older parents to live with the family of the oldest son, my grandparents did not get along with their oldest son's wife and so stayed with us.

I started school in 1947. A few days before the first day of school, I remember becoming very upset because my new textbook was flimsy and of poor print quality, with neither pictures nor a cover. I cried until my mother made a cover and drew a picture of red tulips with the sun shining on them. She made everything we wore in those days—dresses, trousers, slips, even underpants. As far as I can remember, during my childhood, all of her time was occupied by the essential tasks of a homemaker. She spent a full hour preparing breakfast every day. Rooms and hallways had to be dusted twice a day in order for us to feel comfortable walking around barefoot. Roads were unpaved, and poorly constructed houses invited dust carried by the wind. In the evening, my mother made a wood fire to heat the bath water. Since we had no refrigerator, shopping for food was also a part of her laborious daily routine.

Unlike the situation for children born a decade later, toys and games were not available unless our parents made them. To compensate for the lack of toys, my friends and I collected candy wrappers of many colors that had been thrown on the street and roamed through local fields to river banks and ponds; these have now completely disappeared. I would often return home at the end of a long summer day to listen to a popular radio drama telling about children in an orphanage who had lost their parents during the war. I felt I was lucky, having both parents alive.

By the time I was a teenager, our material life had improved greatly. My mother no longer sewed all my clothes, because stores had ready-to-wear clothes. She was able to put her surplus energy into her children's education, becoming a forerunner of the "Education Mom" who goads her children into succeeding at school (now a prevalent model in Japan).

My mother, the third of five children, was more ambitious about her children's education than most of my friends' mothers. My engineer father was often absorbed in mathematical texts and never interfered with what she wanted to do, and so my younger brother and I grew up believing in the value of hard work and good grades. A primary concern for us during our early teens was entering a good high school so that we could get into a good college. There was already a popular saying that "Four hours will pass, five hours will fail," meaning that if you studied so hard that you got just four hours of sleep, you would pass the difficult college entrance test. It is strange to recall that neither I nor my mother thought beyond college to what I would do with my education. What motivated my mother in encouraging us to excel at school was a spirit of competition and a vague desire for upward mobility, which had become more prevalent around that time, once mere survival had ceased to be a concern.

The college I eventually attended, Tsuda College,[3] was one of Japan's oldest all-women colleges and had a tradition of enrolling studious, career-minded women. While small, it had produced many leaders in the fields of education and government. Today, more than 30 percent of all Japanese women receive education beyond high school, but in 1954, when I entered the college, only 5 percent of young women did. A college education for a daughter was considered by most parents unnecessary: it did not contribute to a woman's happiness in marriage but could hinder it by making a woman too clever and proud.

Though Tsuda was a private college, tuition was not very high, and I was among more than half of the students who received no-interest government loans that covered much of the expense. Most of us also earned some money tutoring high school students preparing for their college exams. We were often reminded by our professors—most of whom were women (including Americans and Canadians)—that, in the outside world, we women would have to work twice as hard as men if we wanted to accomplish anything.

I left Japan in 1963 to study in the United States because of financial considerations. Having lost my father when I was seventeen and with no financial support then available in Japan for graduate study, I decided to pursue my education with the help of an American couple, a military man and his wife, and a foreign student scholarship from the University of Denver. Not many Japanese traveled abroad in those days. In fact, those permitted to leave Japan were generally businessmen or students with financial sponsors abroad, like myself. Dollars, with an exchange rate of 360 yen per dollar,[4] were scarce, and I left Japan with $200, the amount I was allowed to take out of the country. I had decided to study social work, which I felt was a pragmatic choice.

During my two years in Colorado, I became aware of the economic changes that were occurring back home. A fellow student from Japan who was an economics major showed me some statistics on Japan's economic development. More personal and telling was a remark made by an acquaintance, a Japanese-American, who said her relatives in Japan no longer seemed to appreciate the care packages her family had been sending them since the end of the war.

At the end of 1965, a year after the Tokyo Olympics, I returned home from Colorado with high expectations. In the brightly lit rooms of the office buildings outside the airport, I saw people still working at seven in the evening. The lateness impressed me as peculiar, since I had not seen such a phenomenon during the two years of my stay in the United States. The transformation of Japanese society was obvious everywhere, even though Japan was then in the middle of an economic slump. Increased urbanization, affluence, and sophistication were clearly evident, as was the problem of pollution, especially in industrial cities such as Minamata and Yokkaichi.

I accepted a position as a clinical social worker at a prefectural mental health clinic in Yokohama and later at a rehabilitation center in Tokyo. Various problems with social work in Japan (including the fact that Japanese people are much more reticent than Americans about verbalizing their personal difficulties, leading me to question the applicability of my U.S. training for my Japanese clients) made me seek a permanent return to the United States in 1969.

From that time until 1987, I felt a need to return to Japan for brief visits every few years to reconnect with the land and people. In 1972, I began going to libraries to read Japanese literature, reflecting my need for the same sense of connection. Eventually, I obtained a Ph.D. in Comparative Literature from the University of California at Los Angeles (UCLA). In 1987, with my American husband and two children, I returned to live in Osaka for an entire year; Tomas and Sashya, fifth and third graders then, attended a public Japanese school.

That year, however, brought the end of something. I felt that I had "become American." I seemed to have lost the ability to be socially indirect; I needed to be unduly frank, to speak my mind. I discovered a dislike of Japanese acquiescence ("it can't be helped"), which may be, to some extent, a lubricant in an overcrowded society. I resisted the rigidity of some Japanese teachers about what was "right" for my children—the need for young people to walk to school as a group, for example; I resented finding that one beverage I had sent for a class hike (orange juice!) was, since it was sweet, "not acceptable."

Since that year, I have returned to Japan less frequently, going largely for family reasons, to see my mother and brother. Nonetheless, I continue to be fascinated by—and a critical observer of—Japan's changing faces.

1

Marriage

Like most women of her generation, my mother found her husband through a go-between. Her tea-ceremony teacher knew of an eligible young man, the brother of one of her students. After both families had a chance to investigate each other's background and the suitability of the prospective couple, the two met briefly on a few occasions; they agreed to the marriage. Their go-between did not know them well (particularly the groom-to-be) and felt little responsibility beyond facilitating the initial communication between the two families. As my mother told me years later, she and her new husband, who was an unusually quiet man, remained silent the whole time on the train ride to the hot springs resort where they spent their honeymoon. This was in 1937, and theirs was a typical *miai* arranged marriage.

Miai literally means "mutual looking." In those days, all men and women were expected to marry, unless they had serious physical disabilities, but the union was not necessarily based on attraction. People believed that, if the match was a good one, conjugal love would eventually develop. "You'll adjust sooner or later and learn to get along," my mother used to say. My parents' marriage was considered successful by the standards of the time because my father was a responsible breadwinner and my mother a capable homemaker. They fulfilled their responsibility of procreation by producing two children and went about their separate activities, which took much of their time and energy. They were reasonably happy (or succeeded in convincing themselves that they were). If they were unhappy, they did not let others know.

The institution of marriage was a family matter, rather than a personal one in Japan from medieval times. It was intended to join two families in an advantageous union and produce children. Confucian teaching maintained that males and females should be separated socially, even in educational institutions, after age seven. Because young people had little opportunity to meet members of the opposite sex of similar class and background, individuals had to rely on *miai* matchmaking to find a partner.

There was, however, a minority of individuals who did not follow this tradition. Beginning in the late 1920s, a few young Japanese, under the influence of Western customs, began to choose marriage partners without family intervention, relying on their own judgment and on a romantic or sexual attraction. One of my mother's two brothers chose his wife on his own and married a young woman he often saw on his way to school. These marriages were called *jiyū kekkon*, or "free marriages," and later, *ren'ai kekkon*, or "love marriages."

Encouraged by individualism, which became more widely accepted after World War II, *ren'ai* marriages gained in popularity. The legal definition of marriage also changed. Instead of being considered an arrangement between families, as the prewar civil codes had prescribed, the 1947 constitution defined marriage as a union "based only on the mutual consent of both sexes." The constitution also stated that the "choice of spouse . . . shall be enacted from the standpoint of individual dignity and the essential equality of the sexes."[1]

Soon the Japanese, particularly young people, began intensely debating the matter of *miai* versus *ren'ai* marriage. I, for one, spent hours discussing the pros and cons of both systems with my friends during my high school days.[2] Love marriage signified for us a youthful rebellion against parental authority and all "feudalist sentiment," as we referred to the establishment. Around this time, I also recall hearing on the radio (and later on television) the ubiquitous question: "Were you married through *miai* or *ren'ai*?" On audience participation programs, such as singing contests, this question was inevitably asked when participants were introduced to the audience. Japanese, both young and not-so-young, eagerly debated marriage during the decade after the end of World War II when they were eagerly absorbing a newly introduced "democracy."

Therefore, when the engagement of current emperor Heisei (then Crown Prince Akihito) to Shōda Michiko was announced in 1958, the Japanese people took a particular interest in this news. Ostensibly, the engagement was the result of a romance, not of a traditional *miai*. The couple had met on a tennis court at a resort and supposedly fallen in love. The news media, particularly television (which was developing rapidly around this time), helped to promote this perception of a romantic choice. Wanting to encourage a new image of the royal family, the Imperial Household Agency did not deny any of the media reports.

Newspaper and magazines, particularly those geared toward young women readers, ran a great many articles about the royal pair (and continued to do so as they got on with building their family life). Along with millions of other Japanese, I believed the story of this fairy-tale marriage with a miller's daughter (Michiko's father owned flour mills) transformed into a princess. What was labeled the "Mitchie (an endearment of Michiko) Boom" in fact aroused a distinct feeling among the Japanese that a new era had arrived and that an old feudalistic family system had been firmly put away.[3] Two years before the royal marriage, the government had reported that, based on rapid economic growth, the postwar recovery of Japan was complete, and, in 1960, it announced an economic plan that promised to double individual income and raise living standards to the level of European countries. In concert with these changes in economic life, people were encouraged to abandon old values.

It is possible to say that the concept of *ren'ai* marriage had acquired orthodoxy in Japan by the end of 1950s. Young people now began insisting that *miai* marriages were only for passive men and women incapable of making important decisions on their own. Japanese society started emphasizing the importance of a family life that would allow greater individual freedom and the pursuit of material satisfaction. The new orientation went along with rapid urbanization and the increasing number of nuclear families, and it was expressed in the extremely popular phrase, *mai hōmu shugi*, or "my-homism."

In the extended family, more commonly found in rural Japan, the wife's main function was to bear sons to preserve family continuity. In modern urban marriage, by contrast, more emphasis has been placed on companionship for mutual understanding. The increasing number of women with higher education and of those who work outside the home has also increased the importance of greater communication and companionship in marriage. Many young Japanese, particularly women, seem to think that compatibility in family background and lifestyle, even in a sense of aesthetics, is crucial in choosing mates.

"What is contemporary marriage in Japan like?" David Mura, a third-generation Japanese American, asked in *Turning Japanese: Memoirs of A Sansei* (The Atlantic Monthly Press, 1991). Mrs. Hayashi, a middle-aged Japanese language instructor, summarized for him Japanese marriage today. Many young couples seen in discos and other popular hangouts openly displaying affection and intimacy, she said, do not necessarily get married. College romances will often end when students graduate, and eventually they will meet someone else through a go-between or their parents. A photo, along with a resumé, will be exchanged, and, if the match seems a good prospect, the young people will agree to meet. They date for six months to a year, and, if both agree, they marry.

These marriages might be called *miai-ren'ai*; they are different from the traditional *miai* in the sense that family control is minimal and that the decision tends to be made after many meetings. Nowadays, marriage agencies, equipped with computer technolgoy, can be used (rather than interventions by relatives and friends) to do the initial compatibility matching. It may be hard to tell the difference between *ren'ai* and *miai* marriages, but, according to a 1983 survey, more than two-thirds of couples reported that theirs was a *ren'ai* marriage.[4]

Mura's conclusion that the criterion in choosing a person to marry in Japan today is not romantic love but whether the match is suitable in view of economic, social, and personality compatibility is an accurate summation. According to the above survey, the three most important considerations for marriage mentioned by women respondents were personality, occupation, and income (for men, they were personality, appearance, and age);[5] love or romantic attraction is not a necessary prerequisite. Economic and social stability have traditionally been the primary motivation for marriage for Japanese women. While men found jobs, which usually became lifetime employment, most young women, in an age when the divorce rate was extremely low, chose marriage for lifetime security. Although the majority of young women even then earned wages, they did so only until they got married. This was in part because it was difficult, if not impossible, for women to find work that would make them financially self-support-ing. The frequently used phrase *eikyū shūshoku*, or "lifetime employment," referred to women's primary motivation for marriage.

That phrase has since died out. And yet, so far as one can see from young women who come to marriage agencies today, the goal is still to find a husband who is occupation-ally prestigious and financially secure.[6] Among the wishes that mothers express for their daughters, the foremost has been that they should become "happily married house-wives" (69 percent in one poll[7]). These are the same mothers who offer specific careers (engineering and government work being the top two choices in the above poll) for their sons' desirable future direction.

Although *ren'ai* marriage has become preferred among young Japanese and *miai* marriage has changed its tradi-tional form somewhat, the *miai* arrangement has survived and continues to be practiced today. A good example of this situation appears among farmers in northern Japan. Unmar-ried men ages twenty-five to thirty-nine (there were 120 of them in 1988) in Higashi-Iriayama, a village in Tokushima Prefecture with a population of 3,000, for example, had difficulty in finding wives. With the intervention of village elders, therefore, they resorted to finding their partners among women from neighboring Asian countries.[8] The severe population imbalance in these remote villages de-rives partly from the fact that young women tend to flee their native villages as soon as they graduate from high school, seeking greater freedom (and husbands) in cities. Knowing that the very existence of their villages depended on finding brides for their bachelors, elders in some villages (and later, publicly run marriage agencies) ventured into "importing" brides from abroad; others sent a group of young men to the Philippines for a group *miai*. Cross-cultural marriage is something that few Japanese had ever expected to see take place. The openness shown by Japanese farmers who have

welcomed brides from beyond national and ethnic boun-
daries transcends their cultural orientation; it shows their
flexibility to adjust the tradition to meet a new reality.

The difficulties faced by urban Japanese men—little time
or opportunity to develop relationships—are actually not so
different from the problems that confront the farmers, and
many young men (and women) in large cities seem to feel
the need for arranged marriage as well. In recent years,
when Japan has had nearly 2 million more single men than
women between ages twenty and thirty-nine, men are particularly feeling the pressure. The marriage agency business
is flourishing, and nearly 70 percent of the clients are male.[9]
In fact, the need for matchmaking services is so great that
some companies include them as a part of their employee
services.[10]

It seems that many men who use marriage agency services want as their future wives women who are both
independent and accommodating, not submissive and
lacking in self-reliance; they expect a wife, more than anything else, to preserve a stable home environment. Women
approach spouse hunting differently. Young city women in
particular now seem to be highly critical of the men around
them.[11] Since most women see home as the area where they
can realistically hope to exercise control, they want to find
mates who will allow them to lead the life they desire. By
asking questions with a certain objectivity, these women
try to make sure that they can eventually lead an enjoyable
and materially comfortable life; they do not hesitate to
shop around, either.

Many women even give an impression that they approach
marriage in the same manner as they do catalogue shopping
for name brands. In a 1985 poll,[12] 100 unmarried women (all
in their mid-to-late twenties and working in central Tokyo)
gave responses that can be reduced to one profile for "an
ideal mate": the prospective husband is four years older
than his wife and has at least a bachelor's degree, preferably

in engineering; he is a *sarariman* with a monthly income of about 350,000 yen ($2,800); he must be at least 170 centimeters (5 feet 8 inches) tall with a lean or medium build; although he may be the oldest son, he should not be the only child (since that would mean the future wife would be solely responsible for his parents in their old age).

The dynamics of contemporary Japanese marriage might be symbolized by a pair of tea cups I saw in the late 1970s in a Tokyo store. These cups, called *myōto jawan*, usually come in two sizes, the large one for the man and the smaller one for the woman. The pair I spotted were of equal size. What caught my attention, besides the equal size, was the writing on each cup, under the headings "Ideal Husband" and "Ideal Wife." "Doesn't forget to smile yet can be tough when necessary," "Enjoys his work but also helps to create harmony at home," and "Able to tell his wife's wishes without their being spelled out" were the top three qualities of an "ideal husband." An ideal wife, on the other hand, was one who "quickly learns the likes and dislikes of her husband," "Is cheerful, charming, but also gentle and obedient," and "Retains a subtle naiveté." Undermining the message implied by the equal size of the man's and woman's cups, the writing represents a traditional notion of the gender relationship in Japanese marriages. In particular, they declare that what men have wanted in a wife is subservience and obedience. Interestingly, Japanese husbands today also want to find in their wives charm and nonthreatening companionship, something men of my father's generation would not admit. According to the teacup, women desire something quite different: they want their husbands to be both tough and gentle, to work hard but also to be family men. Judging from the two lists, husbands are slightly more demanding than wives.

The dynamics of marital relationships are very much culturally determined. The Japanese notion of successful interaction is different from the American one. In 1981, a cross-cultural study that compared 100 American couples living in Kōbe with Japanese couples showed this difference.[13] The majority of American wives thought no leadership was necessary in marriage, while their Japanese counterparts considered male leadership important. The study also found that American husbands saw the ideal wife as cheerful and sociable; she was broad-minded and willing to help her husband's career. To describe "ideal wives," most of the Japanese husbands, by contrast, opted for the much less specific description of "good wife and wise mother," a widely used term with a touch of Confucian doctrine, expressing ideal womanhood.

Another phrase often used by the Japanese husbands was to say that the ideal wife has "an existence like water or air." Reflected in this expression is an attitude of non-commitment and passivity. It implies that the Japanese husband wants his wife to exist as a constant but without too strong an impact, like air. At the same time, she is, again like water and air, crucially important for his survival. My Japanese feminist friends maintain that this desire among Japanese husbands is related to their relationship with their mothers (I myself think this is not a uniquely Japanese trait). Japanese mothers' traditional practice of preferential treatment for sons (upon whom mothers felt they had to depend in their old age) has not changed much over the years; whatever changes have been made are now counterbalanced by tendencies toward overprotectiveness—encouraged by both the decreasing number of children per family and the importance of a mother's role in the son's ordeal of the "entrance examination" (more in Chapter 4). After they marry, many men continue to look for a perpetual caretaker-mother in the wife.

Despite the impact of the many social and economic changes that have affected Japanese marriages, the dynamics between the wife (both *sengyō shufu*, or full-time housewives, and working wives) and the husband remain basically the same. Survey after survey confirms that the majority of the Japanese believe in gender-role division, whereby the marriage partners live in the worlds that are kept separate by their distinctive roles—work and home (more in Chapter 2).

There is no doubt, however, that Japanese wives have become aware of the dead-end aspect of a marriage with rigid role division. Many have left home to go to work; an increase in the divorce rate among middle-aged women is not unrelated to this phenomenon (more in Chapter 3). More than a few Japanese feminists whom I met during 1987 claimed that the rigid gender-role division—not only in households with a full-time housewife, but also among working couples—continues to be practiced and is at the core of many problems. A novel by Kojima Nobuo, entitled *Hōyō kazoku* (*Embracing Family*), symbolically portrays this situation of Japanese couples. Published in 1965, the book delves into the nature of the difference between a husband's and a wife's perception of a marriage—a difference that is extremely subtle and yet seemingly irreconcilable, a schism that has become more clear during the last few decades as Japanese women have become more conscious of their own wishes and power.

Shunsuke, the quintessential Japanese husband of the posteconomic growth era and the protagonist of *Embracing Family*, realizes after the death of his wife, Tokiko, that he cannot live without a *shufu* (housewife), and he frantically tries to replace her. Tokiko, a controlling woman, had been a mother figure to him, something as "essential as water or air." Tokiko had slept with a young American (a symbol of the outside forces that have brought many changes into the Japanese life), but when her fling was found out, she told her husband: "You shouldn't act like that." Tokiko is the antithesis of a submissive and reticent woman, the Japanese stereotype. Nonetheless, Tokiko is also trapped in the idea of marriage with gender-based role division. Possibly a very

of marriage with gender-based role division. Possibly a very
capable woman, she is narrowly defined, by both her husband and society, as a homemaker. Deprived of wider opportunities, she takes lessons in ballroom dancing and has
cosmetic surgeries; when those do not make her content, she
attempts to introduce something totally new into her life—
an American lover. After all of this, however, she finds that
her body has been invaded by cancer.

That the publication of this novel was an epoch-making
event in the history of modern Japanese fiction lies in the
fact that its protagonist, a man with intellect, a respectable
social position, and earning power, is presented as an
individual who lacks basic self-confidence and feels totally
helpless in the face of loss. Attributing a passive or ir-
responsible attitude to Japanese husbands alone would be
one-sided. This, too, is hinted at in *Embracing Family*. Like
Tokiko, Japanese wives may not be emotionally committed
to their marriages. The phrase "A husband is better healthy
and away from home" reflected such an attitude in wives
and was popularized by a television commercial in the
early 1970s. It says that a wife does not need to have a
spouse in her day-to-day life; it is his durability as a breadwinner that is important. Tokiko in fact makes a comment
to Shunsuke to this effect, urging him to think only about
work and bringing home money. Even though she intui-
tively rejects the housewife role assigned to her, she cannot
see herself beyond that role.

There is one aspect of gender-role division that Japanese
wives seem to enjoy—autonomy within the household and
the power that comes with it. Among my Japanese acquaintances are quite a few wives who firmly believe in this
separatist approach (there is minimal verbal communication between the wife and husband in their daily lives,
since it is not needed). Some of the wives I know claim that
they are better off than their more socially emancipated
Western counterparts. They point out their position of

thus control the household. A 1982 survey substantiated this belief, showing that, in more than half of the households studied, the wives controlled family finances (53.8 percent, in contrast to 10.3 percent of households where the husbands were in control).[14] Another aspect was confirmed by a cross-cultural study that compared married couples in Kōbe with couples in Detroit; this study showed that the number of wives who made domestic decisions independently of their husbands was far larger (more than double) in Japan than what it was in the United States.[15] This study also indicated different perceptions between Japanese and American couples regarding gender-based practices at home. For example, while American husbands almost unanimously agreed that they should help with the chores around the house, fewer than half of the Japanese husbands felt that way. Similarly, the majority of American couples considered the discipline of children to be the responsibility of both parents, but only half the Japanese mothers concurred. We can surmise from this poll that, for American couples, a good marital relationship is based on cooperation without leadership, but, for the Japanese, the relative autonomy of wife and husband in their respective areas of responsibility is important. Gender-based role division, widely practiced among Japanese couples, reflects this perception of the marital relationship. The Japanese approach to marriage, then, is that of separatism, with authority exercised by both husband and wife but in different spheres.

It should be noted, however, that the Japanese wife's managing of the household budget is not a practice rooted in tradition, as many seem to think; rather, the custom became widespread, particularly in middle-class households, as recently as the post-World War II period. In those days of economic hardship, wives played a critical role in sustaining the basic economic life of their families by, for instance, making trips to the countryside to obtain food, as my mother did. Even when the immediate postwar period ended, wives continued in this role in cases where the money brought home by husbands was barely enough to provide for families and thus required the careful budgeting of full-time homemakers. Even when general economic conditions improved, the practice of a wife's managing the family budget continued, as I saw in my mother's case; she did not feel that she had to consult with her husband in most decision making, and when she bought something for my brother or me, she simply made us report afterward to my father, who did not seem to care to know.

During the period of rapid economic growth, the division of gender roles became even more firmly established. When husbands found themselves working long hours in pursuit of economic "miracles," it made sense to give wives budgetary control along with other household responsibilities. In a recent nationwide survey (1993), the notion of rigid gender roles expressed in the phrase "men work outside and women keep house" remained well entrenched, being supported by three-fifths of all surveyed.[16]

The wife's household autonomy is more or less guaranteed in this clear division of labor, and it does appear that she enjoys the power. This power, however, is delegated by her husband, rather than inherently belonging to her. Thus, while making all the day-to-day decisions on their own, some wives feel they have to ask their husbands for permission to do volunteer activities or get a part-time job. Furthermore, a wife may have little to say about how her husband spends his time outside the home and how he makes important choices that will affect household finances. Without financial independence, her options are in fact quite limited. Although certainly not so true as in the past, the saying "A wife's freedom is in the palm of her husband" still describes the Japanese wife's position most of the time.

Even with a major increase in Japanese women's earning power in recent years, there are still many wives who do not feel confident enough to be out on their own in the world or to insist on their own agenda. Others conclude that, even with limited autonomy, it is wiser to remain at home. And some remain ambivalent; they seem to fluctuate between independence and a fear of the responsibility. Like women elsewhere, more Japanese wives are now trying to make many difficult decisions as choices become more available to them. A small column in the *Asahi Shimbun* (9 February 1994) reported on the most recent trend of highly diversified life and choice—marriage as well as remaining single—for women in Japan today.

Japanese women now marry at a later age than their mothers did (the average age at which women marry rose from 23.0 to 25.8 between 1910 and 1990; in 1970, 75 percent married before they turned twenty-six, but in 1989, fewer than 45 percent did so). They no longer need to be concerned with being in a "Christmas Cake" situation, a Japanese joke for those who are, like a Christmas cake, without value after twenty-five (Japanese buy a cake for Christmas on 25 December). The number of women who marry for the first time after age thirty has more than doubled in the last two decades. A survey by the Ministry of Health and Welfare's Institute of Population Problems, conducted in 1982 found that 23.6 percent of single women aged thirty to thirty-four said they preferred not to marry at all.

The social stigma previously attached to the unmarried is slowly on its way out as the number of women who stay single, as well as the number of divorcees, has increased. More recently, young women, particularly those who enjoy a good income, have shown an increased reluctance to jump into marriage, a phenomenon termed by the news media the "don't-want-to-get-married syndrome." Accordingly, the terms that people use to refer to unmarried women have undergone changes. A clearly derogatory term, *ōrudo misu* (old miss), was replaced in the late 1960s by a new term, *hai misu*, or high (aged) miss. The newer term implied that being unmarried was a choice. When this term too took on a negative connotation, being used to refer, for example, to Akiko Okumura, who extorted a large sum of money from the bank where she worked in order to please her young lover, yet another word emerged. This term, *shinguru* (single), again an import from English (more often referring to women), revealed greater tolerance for being unmarried. *Shinguru*, in fact, conveys a sense of independence behind the woman's choice. The general sentiment that bachelors, lacking the experience of heading a household, cannot assume managerial responsibility and therefore are not expected to get very far up the corporate ladder is also fading.

Female characters in fiction by women writers during the 1980s are often radically different from those in earlier works. The woman protagonist of "Sinking Ground" by Masuda Mizuko (translated and compiled by Tanaka Yukiko in *Unmapped Territories: New Women's Fiction from Japan*, 1991), for example, is a single working woman who is content living alone in her apartment, her castle; she is more independent-minded than her counterparts in the 1970s fiction (see Chapter 2) and refuses to make tea for a male work colleague. It is not that she does not consider marriage at all, but rather she feels that making her present life solid and satisfying is more important. Another story, "A Straw Dog," by Tomioka Taeko, depicts a single woman who, in her middle age, seduces and uses younger men for sex in order to test her sense of female self. Marriage does not occur to her even as a possibility.

Japanese women today, in fact, feel much less pressure to marry than older generations. A 1990 survey by the Prime Minister's Office showed that more than half of the respondents (women age twenty and older) felt that remaining single was an acceptable option; of this group, those younger than thirty particularly held a nontraditional notion about marriage (only one-quarter of the respondents stated that marriage was necessary). Reflecting this emerging sentiment about marriage among young women in Japan is a dramatic increase in the number of those between ages twenty-five to twenty-nine who are single. These women think that they should not be easily persuaded, and they do not need to marry if they are financially (and psychologically) independent. While women of my mother's generation still firmly believe (according to more than two-thirds of the respondents in the above survey) that women's happiness lies in marriage, some young women today—like Fukuda Yoko, a twenty-seven-year-old licensed pharmacist I met in 1987, for example—consider marriage not essential.

Fukuda has set her own conditions for agreeing to marriage, and these include that she be able to continue working, that her husband accept the frequent traveling required by her job, and that she not live with his parents. She found a man who agreed to these conditions, but, when his parents insisted and he concurred that she should quit working when she had a child, she broke off the engagement. At her parents' urging, Fukuda has met with three prospective suitors since then, but she has yet to find a man who will marry her and accept all of her conditions. Meanwhile, she prefers to stay single rather than compromise. More young women in Japan now try to fit marriage into their long-range career goals, rather than changing their lifestyle in order to be married. Some conclude that marriage and motherhood would cut short their careers. Fukuda is not an exception, as shown in the caption of a weekly magazine that caught my eye recently: "Attaining Independence in Male-Dominated Japan: Women Are Now Choosing a Life without a Partner." A single woman today can buy a house on her own[17] and invest for her retirement, the article explained; she can even dare to have a child alone.

Single motherhood in Japan first caught the attention of the news media during the 1970s; it was practiced by a movie star and was one of the ultimate ways to demonstrate a woman's sense of independence. Both because of the centuries-old Japanese practice of family registration, which keeps a record of a person's antecedents in *koseki*, and because an illegitimate child confronts strong social discrimination, a single woman indeed dares much to have a child even now. Registry with a stamp of illegitimacy would work against the child throughout his or her life, since the *koseki* is used throughout life as an official document needed for entering school, obtaining a passport, and even for getting a job. According to journalist Yoshihiro Kiyoko, who interviewed unmarried women in 1987, the family registration system was a major factor preventing single women from becoming mothers; if they gave in to their wish, it was against strong pressure from their parents to have abortions. The birth rate outside marriage in Japan is the lowest in the world.[18]

Not registering a marriage is another phenomenon observed in recent years in Japan. This is a choice women (and men) are resorting to in protest against the double standard clearly seen in the current family registration system. In order to register a marriage in this system, couples must designate the head of the household, and, while the full name of the household head (almost always a male) is written into the *koseki* registry, his wife, and later, his children, are entered without surnames.[19] Demanding that a couple have the same surname is increasingly problematic for women, particularly for professional women.

An increasing number of women have expressed their objections to the family registry because it suggests that they and children are merely appendages. Some, therefore, resort to remaining single on paper; they feel that keeping their maiden name is part and parcel of their liberation from male-centered practices in marriage.[20] To persist in this resistance, however, can be quite tricky, as my friend Inoue Haruyo learned.

In her first marriage, Haruyo took her husband's family name without question, following common practice. Upon her divorce, she took back her maiden name, as the law then demanded.[21] When Haruyo married a second time, her husband agreed to adopt her surname, Inoue, so that the name of her son by her first marriage (who adopted Haruyo's name upon her divorce) could be the same as that of his parents. This seemed a good solution until recently, when her husband had to go abroad on an assignment. Having legally changed his name but kept his old surname for professional use, Haruyo's second husband had to gain his own surname back in order to avoid unnecessary confusion and red tape expected during his trip (the name on his passport is not the same name by which he is known professionally).

Facing this situation, Haruyo filed another "divorce," this time a "paper divorce," as she called it. When she explained at the family registry office why the "new address" on the form requesting divorce was the same as the "old address," the angry clerk threatened not to process her divorce, since the couple would continue to live together. The registry officer's attitude, Haruyo thinks, represents the disapproving attitude of the average Japanese.

Haruyo is among a growing number of women in Japan who are taking various actions to counter male-centered practices concerning marriage. Reflecting an increasing interest in changing the registry system and allowing marriage partners to have different surnames, the government formed a committee in January 1991, to study the issue. Being able to choose their names upon marriage has a symbolic significance for women's independence in Japan; many are concerned with inevitable difficulties, such as problems in choosing children's names and discord between young couples and their parents.

Japanese women in general are more willing to examine the tradition of marriage in all of its aspects, and some are seeking ways to find fulfillment in a new context. Meanwhile, traditional practice of *miai* continues in different forms to meet the demands of new realities. Some people still accept the age-old notion that women's happiness lies in marriage.

2

Wives

Japanese businessmen may work twelve hours a day and do "business socializing" at bars after work and on the golf course on Sundays. As a result, some of their wives experience "an inconsolable sense of loneliness and futility." This is the conclusion of Saitō Shigeru, the author of *Shishūki no tsumatachi* (*Wives in Their Autumnal Days*), a much discussed book published in 1982.

Saitō maintains that a Japanese husband who is a corporate employee can work as long and as hard as he wishes at his job because his wife raises the children, keeps his house, and attends to his daily needs with a degree of professional competence. Men, in other words, "hire" wives as their "caretakers" so that they themselves can perform at full capacity in the corporate world. As some Westerners have observed, the high productivity and economic strength of Japan have thus been achieved in part through sacrifices by the wives of "corporate soldiers." Saitō, a reporter for the Kyōdo News Service, in fact began his research intending to write a book about corporate soldiers but ended up writing about their wives.

The phrase "corporate soldiers on the front line and their wives behind them" was popularized by journalists around the time Saitō's book came out. This pattern among Japanese couples is exemplified by the Yamadas, whose story appeared in a newspaper column.[1] The Yamadas were one of many couples who single-mindedly fulfilled their respective responsibilities during the era of economic expansion. Yamada Yoshiko admitted that she married her husband, nearly three decades earlier through a *miai* arrangement, because he seemed to be a good provider, ambitious and hard-working. He was indeed committed to his work, making it necessary for Yoshiko to raise three children virtually by herself and to perform all of the expected familial duties, including taking care of her in-laws.

Yoshiko was among the increasing number of patients receiving treatment at private psychiatric clinics. She had been suffering for some time from insomnia and a total lack of interest in housework. She also had stiffness around her neck and shoulders; her body felt as if it were being tightly squeezed, as in an iron ring. She could not think of any reason why she should feel the way she felt. Her husband held an important position at his company, and together they had acted as "go-betweens" for as many as ten young couples. Her grown children were all healthy and successful.

Yoshiko's "corporate soldier" husband did not hide his annoyance when he came into the psychiatric clinic after urging by the counselor. For the previous forty years, he stated, he had thought about nothing but his work: "Even in the bathroom I was thinking about the problems I had to deal with at work." He had been so busy that he often wished "a tablet or two" would take care of the business of eating. He stated that he was happy being able to work without worrying about his home or family; he also told his subordinates that their duty was to the company, not their families. His company had rewarded his devotion with slow but steady promotion. He was content, and he did not understand what was wrong with his wife.

Mr. Yamada may represent a type of corporate soldier whose numbers will steadily decline in Japan for a variety of reasons.[2] Nevertheless, one can see the problems he might pose for a wife. Another woman in a situation similar to Yoshiko's described her relationship with her corporate soldier husband this way: "He is going up in the escalator while I'm going down."

Loneliness, doubts about their marriages and relationships with their husbands, and even self-loathing characterize the inner lives of the women depicted in the fiction compiled in *This Kind of Woman: Ten Stories by Japanese Women Writers, 1960–1976* (edited by Tanaka Yukiko and Elizabeth Hanson, 1982). The central characters' secret yearnings and strong ambivalence about their roles (as in "Luminous Watch," "Last Time," and "The Man Who Cut the Grass"), their self-hatred, which pushes them into exploring their past and repressed emotions ("A Bed of Grass" and "Family in Hell"), and even their sense of precariousness, accompanied by the feeling that they might do something outrageous, even go mad ("Doll Love" and "The Three Crabs")—these are all fictional representations of the experiences of women like Yamada Yoshiko.

In Japan as elsewhere, alcohol offers one form of escape. During the 1980s, the term *kicchin dorinkā*, or kitchen drinker, began appearing in Japanese newspaper and magazine articles, and one study showed a dramatic increase in the number of older alcoholic women. Alcoholism among Japanese women has become as much a problem as it is in Western countries.[3]

Compared with American couples, there is a high degree of emotional autonomy in Japanese conjugal relationships, making it hard, particularly for Westerners, to see that a couple is truly married. Referring to the miniscule amount of time that Japanese couples spend together, as shown in a

1987 study by the Committee on Contemporary Society and Sex, a French correspondent, for instance, wrote: "They certainly have sexual intercourse, but other types of communication are totally absent."[4] A similar opinion was expressed by a Canadian journalist, who speculated upon why the divorce rate was relatively low in Japan: "The truth of the matter is that Japanese couples are divorced in reality [according to Western standards] even though they are married on paper."[5]

These statements may be exaggerated; it is also clear that the tides are shifting. Young couples are now frequently seen shopping together in supermarkets and department stores, and some fathers are willing to reserve Sundays as "family day" to take their wives and children for outings. But the lack of conjugal intimacy among the Japanese continues to affect them and can be seen in regard to such matters as birth control.

According to sociologist Samuel Colman, Japanese couples find it difficult to take the initiative in using effective birth control methods, because conjugal sexuality—like emotional intimacy—is deemphasized in Japanese culture.[6] In view of the absence of religious opposition to birth control, this assessment seems accurate; one study showed that slightly fewer than half of the couples surveyed practiced birth control.[7] Since birth control pills are not available in Japan (the government does not approve their sale for safety reasons), those couples who do practice birth control rely on condoms (most frequently), intrauterine devices (IUDs), or the rhythm method. When these methods fail or when no method is used, abortion becomes the route to birth control.

The above-mentioned study on marital sex among Japanese couples includes a section on abortion, showing that a high percentage of wives of managerial-level corporate employees (64.1 percent of the respondents) had had at least one abortion. While it is well known that abortion is widely practiced in Japan, what is not so well known is that this is a relatively recent development. When the Eugenic Protection Law was amended in 1949, it included generous provisions to allow for abortions under a variety of conditions. The reason of "economic hardship" continues to be used by women seeking an abortion (giving a reason is required by law). Most Japanese seem to approve of abortion if there are medical or economic reasons.[8] A Buddhist ceremony exists to help relieve the guilt women may suffer over abortion, and some temples capitalize on this situation by offering, for a fee, special services for unborn fetuses.

Despite a steady decrease in the number of children that Japanese couples are willing to have (the family fertility rate dropped to 1.4 children per family in 1992), marital sex continues to be viewed as being primarily for reproduction. This may be a reason why Japanese marital sex has its problems; this was the conclusion of the above-mentioned study by the Committee on Contemporary Society and Sex. The study showed, for instance, that among nearly all of the respondents it was the husband who initiated sex. While the large majority of wives (88 percent) agreed that sex was an important factor in their marriages, half of them said they would not tell their husbands when they failed to gain satisfaction. One might conclude from these figures that many Japanese wives still approach sex with a sense of duty and loyalty.

Despite a persistent sexual double standard that permits a husband extramarital affairs while a wife is expected to remain entirely faithful, Japanese women have recently become more open about their needs and about their perceptions of marital sex. According to Tamura Masaaki of Sitama University Medical School, some basic changes can be observed in the sexual morality of Japanese wives. Wider acceptance of *furi sekkusu* ("free sex," meaning extramarital sex) is one of these changes. Although shocking to more traditional-minded Japanese, only one-third of the wives surveyed in Tamura's study disapproved of the "free sex" trend. The number of those who approved of extramarital sex was even larger when it was "based on mutual affection."

Furthermore, information on commercialized sex and other sexually explicit materials proliferate in any large city in Japan today. Foreign tourists may be shocked to see, for example, the abundance of large movie posters depicting virtually naked women and other blatant displays on busy downtown streets. On commuter trains, it is common to see both young and middle-aged men reading sports newspapers with large-size photos of explicitly sexual, and often sexually violent, acts. One could speculate about the need that this material fills in a culture where some wives refer to their husbands as "my boarder."

For some wives, husbands are absent more frequently than daily and during business hours. *Tanshin funin*, or unaccompanied transfer, in which employees move to another city to work and leave their families behind, has become an object of social concern as its frequency has increased. In late 1987, the number of corporate employees who lived and worked away from their families was estimated to be about 170,000. If overseas transfers are included, the number is even larger.

The term *tanshin funin* did not even exist twenty-five years ago. In the past, one of the few reasons that married men left their families for an extended period was to go abroad to study. For financial reasons (stipends were not given to wives or other family members), it was accepted that men would leave their families behind. In 1964, I met a few of these Japanese husbands spending their second and even third year on an American university campus away from their wives. I did not sense much anxiety among these men over the extended separation. My American friends could not understand it.

In today's Japan, a common reason for a wife's not moving with her husband may include the children's education (more in Chapter 4). To relocate the family and change a child's school can indeed be detrimental under the present entrance examination system. Other reasons include the lack of adequate housing and concerns for aged parents' difficulty in adjusting to a new neighborhood. Dual careers, perhaps the only conceivable reason for American couples to consent to living apart, are not a factor in unaccompanied transfers. Although the number of women working outside the home is on the rise, the number of two-career couples is still quite small in Japan.

Tanshin funin is sometimes simply part of company policy. Using the rationale that some underdeveloped countries are too dangerous for women and children to live there, some companies make it a policy to transfer male employees alone.[9] One survey showed a surprisingly high degree of tolerance among the wives: 20 percent of those polled confessed anxiety over the extended separation, but 43 percent stated that the separation was not damaging to their marriage.[10]

A husband and father's extended absence from home is not normal; it does cause a great deal of stress, as well as practical problems for those left behind. It is a trying experience for the husband as well. Returning each night to a dark room where no meal is waiting is depressing, said a newspaper columnist in his fifties. He wrote about a new adult toy, a doll dressed in a kimono, who, when tapped on her knee, uttered wifely phrases: "Good-bye. Come home early, please" and "You've got everything? A handkerchief? Your wallet?" According to a survey by the Prime Minister's Office, more than half of all company employees in their thirties and forties wish not to be transferred.

Tanshin funin is only one of many causes of the increasing instability of the Japanese family, which has been observed for some time now. While the Japanese are doing better now in health, environment, economic stability and community involvement, studies have shown that they feel hard-to-solve problems lie in family and education. A 1984 poll by the Prime Minister's Office, for example, found that only half of the families surveyed ate dinner together on a regular basis; nearly one-fourth felt little or no family togetherness at mealtime. A 1983 study by the Prime Minister's Office also showed a clear decline in the number of people who felt satisfied with their daily family life.

Japanese family life has undoubtedly changed during the past decade or two, and a new perception of it appears on prime-time television *hōmu dorama*, or home dramas. "Family with unity," an image once central in television shows, has been replaced by families where the parents and children go their separate ways and engage in their own activities. In these dramas, communication among family members is often poor, and the family as a whole seems to be in deeper trouble than previously, with complex problems. Extramarital affairs among couples who are separated by *tanshin funin* are also dramatized on the screen.

Japanese television home dramas have recently begun representing the lives of women much more candidly. Central female characters now tend to live for their own personal pursuits, rather than for the sake of family, and married women are depicted not primarily as mothers, but as wives. The wives are more assertive than those of earlier family dramas, and they are far more demanding; they even fall in love with men other than their husbands and seek divorce if necessary. Conflicts between wives and husbands, as well as those between couples and their parents, are now presented on the screen without illusions or optimism.

The situations shown in an enormously popular drama series called *Kinyōbi no tumatachi e* (*For Friday's Wives*) are complex indeed; they include extramarital affairs, separation, divorce, and single motherhood. Women in this drama live with greater freedom and responsibility for themselves. It is from this series that the term *kintsuma* (shortened from the title) was coined, referring to the more independent or daring housewives of the 1980s.

Married women in these television dramas are often presented as having lasting friendships with other women, which almost never occurred in earlier dramas. Four central characters in "Falling in Love" (a part of *For Friday's Wives*), for example, are good friends who have maintained contact since their graduation from junior college. Of the four major characters in "Falling in Love," only one woman, who lives with her family and her mother-in-law, fits the traditional mold; the others include a divorced woman running a bistro and raising a son, a woman married but separated from her husband, who has been transferred to another city, and a single working woman. The plot is complicated by the fact that the single woman is the former lover of the first woman's husband.[11]

Television dramas no longer tout the traditional idea that a woman's happiness is found only within the home and a satisfactory marriage. In addition to new messages conveyed through their characters and their opinions, popular television dramas of the 1980s, such as *For Friday's Wives*, feature new lifestyles—nice houses, trendy clothes, and interesting jobs. While they feature women who are not just mothers and wives, they tend to focus on the more fashionable and superficial aspects of a contemporary woman's life. Suggesting that the extent of women's self-realization is limited, the shows do not really explore how or why. Thus, they fail to create useful role models for Japanese women viewers who want to go beyond rebellion or fantasy.

In real life as well as in television dramas, Japanese wives are more openly expressing their frustration, discontent, and unwillingness to suppress their needs and desires; some are in revolt. This phenomenon does not agree with the traditional image of Japanese women nor with that more recently propagated by Western news media, which portrays Japanese women as a stabilizing force in the society.

The new focus in recent television dramas is no doubt related to the search by Japanese women (wives in particular) for greater independence. Japanese housewives used to be called *okusan*, meaning "one in the back of the house." Housewives today, however, may no longer stay at home. A new image, particularly for younger housewives, is not of a woman who is contented staying at home, satisfied with performing household tasks, and living solely for her family. Rather, this younger housewife frequently leaves her house, to seek opportunities for self-improvement, to network with other women, or simply to have a good time.

In 1987, I witnessed an example of this new development in Osaka, in the penthouse restaurant of the fashionable Hilton Hotel. It was a weekday, and the large restaurant was filled with women in their late twenties and thirties; I could tell they were not meeting for business purposes. In groups of twos or threes, they seemed quite comfortable, enjoying their unhurried, luxurious buffet lunches. Observing a scene I had never before encountered during previous visits to Japan, I recalled that the Japanese tour groups I had seen in Hong Kong a few weeks earlier were also full of women (though those had been mostly middle-aged). It is now not at all uncommon to see women in coffee houses, chatting and relaxing during the day or even at night. Polls show that the nonworking Japanese housewife's free time has steadily increased over the years, reaching seven hours and twenty minutes per day in 1983, a dramatic increase from the three hours and forty-three minutes of 1963.[12]

A Japanese wife's number one virtue used to be skillful management of the household budget, and her overriding concern was to be a careful and wise consumer. She came to be called "Mrs. Automation" when she began enjoying modern household conveniences for the first time. Eventually, the media created the phrase "the three Cs" to indicate her dream: cars, coolers (air-conditioners), and color televisions. For some years now, however, the Japanese wife has not been satisfied with only material goods and has turned to a different set of Cs: culture, creation, and communication. Some prefer studying, sports, and society. This change symbolizes a shift in focus from material satisfaction to personal well-being. In Japan today, full-time housewives without young children and those who work part-time enjoy sports, hobbies, studies, or grass-roots community involvement.

Since 1975, when the United Nations' Decade for Women was declared, the Japanese government has adopted a position of encouraging housewives to become involved in activities, to get out of their houses, and to be socially active. Many community centers that have been built and run by local governments offer adult education classes in such diverse subjects as traditional art and crafts, literature, psychology, and physical exercise.

As a part of an effort to improve their image in the "Age of Women," businesses also encourage women to be active outside the home by sponsoring various cultural and community activities. The major newspapers have daily announcements of seminars, meetings, and special events of all sorts, many of which are geared toward homemakers. A notice about a two-day conference on women's history, which I noticed in a newspaper during a visit to Japan in 1983, is an example. Because child care was offered for the participants, I could tell that this was not a professional meeting. Curiosity led me to attend the conference, and I discovered that it was a gathering of lay historians, most of whom were full-time housewives. I was impressed by the size of the conference and by the high quality of the presentations.

During the 1980s, Japanese women also began showing a greater interest in issues such as women's independence, social changes, and the political process. Neighborhood community centers often supported at least two or three *jishu* (autonomous) groups, which were formed by women themselves, often as the result of a lecture series sponsored by the local government. In 1987, I attended a monthly meeting of one of these groups, where a professor of Japanese literature gave a talk on a feminist interpretation of the work of Natsume Sōseki, whose novels delve into male-female relationships. This led to another session at a nearby restaurant and to more discussion of broader issues confronting Japanese women. "Autonomous" groups differ: Some are reading groups, others share hobbies, but most appear to be conscious of social issues.

Karuchā sentā, or culture centers, became exceedingly popular during the 1980s—a booming industry, in fact. In 1989, the Asahi Culture Center, with its central office in a high-rise building in the heart of Shinjuku, Tokyo, offered 12,000 classes on 470 different subjects, from Flamenco dancing and *sumi* painting to Jungian psychology and English conversation.[13] In its fifteenth year, the center had nine other locations throughout Japan. Eighty percent of the students were women, and of these 60 percent were housewives. Culture centers are unusual in that they neither require entrance tests or certificates of completion nor set age limits, all of which makes studying more accessible and attractive for people like middle-aged housewives. The tuition varies, but generally one three-month class meeting twice a week costs about 20,000 yen ($150), an amount that some housewives can afford without straining their household budgets. It is roughly equivalent to the amount a man might spend in a few hours in a Tokyo bar.

During the 1970s, a Western journalist called Japanese houses "rabbit hutches." Some Japanese realized that the term implied not only to small, crowded living spaces but also to an impoverished state of mind—the habitat for a husband who is not only preoccupied with work but who looks for self-fulfillment through his work only and for a wife who focuses only on her family and relies on someone else for her sense of self-worth. For the majority of Japanese couples, there has been little improvement in living spaces, but wives have learned to get out of their cramped houses and apartments and to be active outside. As the new economic reality of the 1990s set in, husbands have begun (have sometimes been forced) to look to other areas—their homes and children—for a source of satisfaction and a focus for their energy. Japanese couples now, it seems, face the task of learning to establish a more satisfying marriage partnership on a new ground—a ground that appears to be on the horizon.

3

Divorce in Japan

In 1983, there was one divorce for every 4.3 marriages in Japan. Although that was still about half the rate in the United States, the rate doubled from what it had been fifteen years before. The number of divorces has continued to increase during the last decade, and, in 1992, it reached nearly 180,000 cases a year.[1] Along with increased numbers, it is noteworthy that divorces initiated by women, particularly older women, are on the rise. The 1986 census showed that 13 percent of all divorces involved couples who had been married for twenty years or more, a dramatic change considering that divorce among older couples was virtually unheard of in the past.

Until the end of World War II, divorce in Japan was largely a male prerogative. A woman could file for divorce only on the grounds of cruelty, desertion, or serious misconduct— not for infidelity. She, on the other hand, could be divorced and imprisoned for two years for adultery. Since the custody of children was almost always granted to the father, a woman often did not seek divorce even in those limited cases where it could be obtained. Considering this historical background, the recent development of Japanese women initiating divorce proceedings represents a radical change indeed.

A major factor in the steady increase in divorce in Japan has been the rise in women's earning power. Although the majority of Japanese women have worked, traditionally, they were helping their husbands and other male members of the family in farming, cottage industries, or family businesses, a circumstance in which women had no income of their own. As the country's economy moved from an agricultural base to one based on manufacturing and service industries, the opportunities for women to earn income expanded. Nevertheless, since well-paid jobs were extremely limited and women's employment was expected to last only until they found husbands, women were still economically dependent. This dependency was one of the primary incentives for them to marry. During the last few decades, opportunities for women to achieve financial independence have increased, however, and more women have proven to be successful as professionals, earning good salaries.

The fact that Japanese couples are having fewer children has removed another deterrent to divorce. Supporting only one or two children, instead of three or four (the birth rate per woman in 1926 was 5.11, compared to 1.54 in 1990), is less difficult for a divorced mother. In view of the very small proportion of Japanese fathers actually paying child support, this is a significant factor in the increasing divorce rate.

Besides their improved earning power, women's longer life expectancy (now eighty-two for women, seventy-six for men; life expectancy has nearly doubled in half a century) is making Japanese women less willing to endure a troubled marriage.[2] Having finished raising their children and taken dutiful care of their aged parents and parents-in-law, not a small number of women in their fifties and sixties suddenly realize how unsatisfactory their own lives have been. "There must be more to my life," they conclude, and some choose divorce. These women prefer to live alone rather than endure another twenty years or more of certain unhappiness. They sometimes also find that their husbands, now retired and home all day, are a great burden to them.

Another factor behind the rise in the divorce rate is the increased interest among women in pursuing a career. Although the problems of combining the responsibilities of home and work are shared by women in other industrialized countries, in Japan, where a rigid gender division of labor is still widely accepted and practiced, the dilemma is greater. Combining career and family is often not a real option. Consider the case of Mitsuko, a fashion designer in her mid-thirties, whose story of divorce was recounted in the popular women's monthly magazine *Fujin Kōron* (*Women's Forum*, June 1982).

Although her husband understood her need to work and although she loved her son, Mitsuko wanted a divorce. Work was her real life, and she wanted to become a better designer. In recent years, she had felt a surge of creativity, but her sense of duty as a wife and mother seemed to pull her away from her work. Going to a disco with young people, for instance, was part of her professional development as a designer, and yet, on such occasions she could not get rid of the nagging feeling that she was not where she ought to be. When an offer came for her to run a studio, she felt it was a chance she could not pass up. After agonizing for three months, she decided that there was only one way to move forward in her work: a divorce.

Divorce for the sake of mid-career professional advancement and for personal development is something entirely new for Japanese women, and it is still not frequent. Much more common are divorces that take place within the first five years of marriage. In these divorces as well, however, one sees changing attitudes among the Japanese toward marriage and family.

Young people today give the older generations of Japanese the impression that they fall in love quickly, get married right away, and then, when the marriage is in trouble, resort quickly to divorce. Having grown up with greater freedom than earlier generations, they may not believe in the virtues of self-denial or perseverance; unlike their mother's generation, they may feel that their future is entirely in their own hands. The following case, reported in a serialized study of contemporary divorces in *Shūkan Asahi* (*Asahi Weekly*, 6 July–9 September 1984), illustrates this situation.

Midori and her husband, Noboru, began dating in high school and had their first sexual experience together the year they entered college. They later decided to go their separate ways, until they met again at the wedding of a mutual friend; they then decided that they, too, should get married. In the beginning, Noboru was an understanding husband and encouraged Midori to keep her job. With their parents' help, they bought a house in a suburb, and on Sundays they went shopping together, dressed in matching name-brand jeans. Their lifestyle of croissants and coffee for breakfast, of dinner with wine, however, lasted only until their first child was born. Midori stopped working, and Noboru started coming home late. Their sex life began to deteriorate.

One Saturday, Midori suggested an outing, but Noboru "had some work to do." Disgruntled, Midori decided to go alone to a bar that she and Noboru used to frequent, only to discover her husband there, sitting next to another woman. Separation followed, and, eventually, divorce. Midori's major dissatisfaction centered on not being able to enjoy life as she had before marriage. Noboru felt that he should have both the right to work as he wanted and the freedom to spend time away from his family. He was not really interested in the woman sitting next to him at the bar.

Many divorces that take place within the first years of marriage are similar to the case of Midori and Noboru. The partners do not want to give up the freedom and privileges they had enjoyed prior to marriage. Often husbands demand the same treatment they had received from their mothers, but younger wives, who may have grown up with the new idea of equality between men and women, find it difficult to face the gender disparity still permeating Japanese marriages. Furthermore, in a culture where wife and husband rarely function as a couple outside the family, a woman's social and recreational life in Japan, even today, rapidly diminishes after marriage.[3]

A male university professor and author, Ebisaka Takeshi, has made several observations about marriage and divorce in modern Japan.[4] According to Ebisaka, few divorced men can articulate the reasons for their divorce, and this is because they are so "insensitive" to what has happened in their relationship with their wives that they cannot verbalize it. Men more than women, he thinks, stop thinking about the quality of relationship the moment the marriage vows are exchanged, and a husband tends to see his wife primarily as housekeeper and sex partner, as well as wanting her to play the role of mother.

Young women are not entirely without fault, however. Surveys show that in choosing a future husband, women tend to put a high priority on social status, job stability, and physical appearance (see Chapter 1). I am reminded of a phrase, "Narita divorce," which I recently learned from a friend visiting from Japan. One of many media-coined phrases pointing to new social trends, "Narita divorce" refers to those divorces, now not so rare, that take place immediately after the honeymoon. (Many Japanese honeymooners nowadays choose destinations in foreign countries, leaving from and returning to Narita Airport— thus the phrase.) A young wife returns from her honeymoon disillusioned about her husband; he has apparently not achieved emotional separation from his mother, and, though capable, he is more like a robot than a person worthy of her respect, an aspect she had not given much attention prior to marriage.

There are, of course, women who feel that divorce is not an option. This can be seen in the following case study from *Josei no kenri (Women's Rights)*.[5] Fumiko, who had been married for ten years and had two children, discovered that her husband was having an affair with a woman from his office and that the woman was pregnant by him. When she asked her husband to give up the other woman, he not only refused but began living with her for half of every month, giving Fumiko only half his salary.

Because she had no particular job skills, Fumiko could not find any work but stuffing envelopes. Consulting an attorney, she learned that, upon divorce, she was entitled to half the family assets; she also had the right to ask for alimony. Since she and her husband had no savings or property to speak of, however, these resources would not amount to much. Moreover, if Fumiko divorced, she would have to leave the house the family was renting at a cheap rate from one of her husband's relatives. Fumiko's husband was willing to maintain the status quo, as long as she did not object to his selfish arrangement; Fumiko's own parents and siblings were against divorce. Not only would her children suffer emotionally, they told her, but the divorce would be detrimental to the children's future employment and marriage. Fumiko realized that, even though she had the right, she could not divorce.

Madoka Yoriko, who has conducted seminars for women known as "Divorce with a Smile," agrees that there are many women like Fumiko, who cannot divorce primarily for financial reasons. The budgetary constraints on a divorced woman raising children alone are quite severe, in part because of inadequate settlements and the lack of child support, which are common.

That divorce is not as easy as it is made out to be on television dramas is also the opinion of Iijima Kimiko, another woman who has made a business out of a new trend and founded a magazine called *Sutāto* (*Start*), Japan's first magazine devoted to divorce, in early 1984; the first issue of the magazine is said to have sold out immediately. *Start* is targeted at women, and, in addition to case analyses of contemporary breakups, it presents useful information on settlements and on how to prepare for the process. According to Iijima's estimates, in contemporary Japan, there are ten times as many "divorce candidates" as couples who actually divorce.

When a divorce hotline was set up in Tokyo for two weeks in early 1983, 90 percent of the callers were female. The three most common reasons they gave for considering divorce were a husband's extramarital affair, his neglect of family, and financial problems. Different age groups expressed different reasons: Complaints voiced by women callers in their fifties focused mainly on husbands who showed little interest in their families. Women with younger children were usually caught between the desire for a fresh start for themselves and concern for the children, but many seemed to feel strongly that they should postpone divorce until their children reached college age. The major issue facing women callers in their forties was their husbands' infidelity, but other problems, such as alcoholism and physical abuse, were also mentioned. Of all age groups, this last group seemed to be most certain about wanting divorce but found it difficult to agree on terms of custody and child support.[6]

With the increase in divorce over the past few decades, Japanese attitudes toward divorce are slowly but steadily changing. While there was still considerable stigma in 1987, a survey that year showed that 61 percent of the total population (70 percent of women) accepted divorce as a way out of an unsuccessful marriage.[7] When the question was put differently, however, presenting divorce as a positive choice or as a kind of freedom ("If you don't get along with your spouse, is it all right to get a divorce?"), the result was different: only 22 percent of men and women responded favorably. Divorce is most acceptable among working women and among those with higher levels of education. Since the number of Japanese women who receive higher education is increasing, as is the number of working women, divorce is expected to become even more common. As for remarriage, Japanese women are much less inclined to remarry than their American counterparts. A study has shown that only one-third of divorced women (slightly more than half of the men) planned or even wanted to marry again.[8] Third marriages are extremely rare in Japan.

About 90 percent of divorces in Japan are consensual divorces, referred to as *kyogi rikon*. They require only the submission of marriage deregistration papers to a registrar's office. One reason behind the high rate of consensual divorce is privacy, with the reasoning that the negotiations, even with regard to custody and property settlement, should be totally between the parties involved. Even when the breakdown of marriage can be clearly attributed to one party, the majority of these consensual divorces are ultimately filed on grounds of "personality incompatibility." Since these divorces are consensual and are accomplished without a legal battle, couples tend to settle easily on this vague but convenient reason. There is no judicial supervision in these divorce agreements, and they are very simple and quite inexpensive.

Among the reasons given on deregistration papers, sexual problems are suspiciously absent. According to a poll of 2,000 women who attended Madoka's "Divorce with a Smile" seminars, however, such problems are actually one of the major factors leading to divorce.[9] In this inconsistency we see an example of the Japanese reluctance to make private matters public. Other real reasons that wives often give for requesting divorce include physical abuse and extramarital affairs of the husband; the husbands' reasons include the wives not getting along with their in-laws.

When there is no consensual agreement, divorce in Japan can be very difficult. For these divorces, the civil code requires that the petitioning spouse prove that the other party has committed acts of unchastity, has maliciously deserted the spouse, has been missing for at least three years, or has been diagnosed as having irremediable mental illness; it also allows for "a grave reason which makes continuation of the marriage difficult." This "grave reason," however, has strictly excluded causes such as incompatibility, estrangement, or even extended separation. So long as the other party would not consent, divorces for such reasons were impossible until 1987.

In the fall of 1987, the Supreme Court reversed a decision dating from thirty-five years before, granting a divorce to a man who had been separated from his wife for thirty-eight years.[10] This brought Japan closer to endorsing the "no-fault" divorce now common in the United States and other industrialized countries. All in all, this decision was well received by people who have realized for some time that societal and legal pressures have little effect in keeping marriages from breaking down.

The introduction of the "no-fault" approach shows a shift in the Japanese view of marriage. Even if "no fault" divorce is a reasonable position, however, its introduction may have a negative consequence for some wives, considering that there is no community property law in Japan. Some people are also concerned with the subtle psychological effect upon consensual divorces since such divorces are sometimes reached through bullying and intimidation by husbands.

In contested divorces, a family court mediation is mandated prior to litigation. In helping the couple to reach mutual agreement, the court mediators, usually men or women of learning and experience rather than professionals, often discourage divorce if one party is opposed to it. If mediation fails, the case goes to a trial court, where a judge settles the dispute. The number of divorces that reach this level has consistently been very small, about 1 percent of all divorces.

The following case, in which a husband requested divorce on the grounds of his wife's refusal to live with him, illustrates a contested divorce.[11] The husband was transferred to another city but the wife insisted that she had to remain in Tokyo with their son, who was preparing for his university entrance examination. After a few sessions with a family court counselor, the couple agreed to try again to save their marriage. The wife made some attempts to visit her husband in the city where he now worked, but her heart was really with their son. When the husband took the case to district court, this time even more resolved to get a divorce, the wife maintained that her remaining in Tokyo was in fact her duty toward their son, which was hardly grounds for divorce. She also hired a private detective and found out that her husband was involved with another woman.

The court decision, reached three years after the case was filed, rejected the wife's contention that her husband wanted a divorce so he could marry his lover. It also denied the husband's request for custody of the son and ordered him to pay child support of 30,000 yen ($230) a month until his son finished college. Since the couple had maintained two households over a prolonged period, they had no assets to speak of except a house, the title of which was transferred to the wife's name. The husband thus achieved what he originally wanted—a divorce—but at a price.

Studies have shown that only slightly more than half of all consensual divorces included agreements on property division and alimony, and about 60 percent of the wives received little money or property. Even in divorces mediated by family court, the overall picture is not markedly different.[12] In the absence of a community property law, a wife's contribution in helping her husband to accumulate assets does not have to be considered at the time of divorce if the assets are in the husband's name. Still, a wife can keep what she has earned or the money she has saved so long as she has put her resources in her own name. When no judicial supervision is provided, as in consensual divorces, women are obviously at a disadvantage, since gender-role separation has strongly encouraged wives to stay home without their own income. Considering that, in 1985, the average settlement for women was as low as 3.36 million yen ($22,000) in divorces mediated by family courts, this is a legitimate concern.

Since the custody of children is now given more often to mothers (unlike the pre-World War II practice) and since fathers often do not pay child support, one of the biggest problems caused by divorce in Japan, as elsewhere, is the financial hardship it imposes on women. Mothers who already have good jobs at the time of divorce are rare, while those who end up working at two or three part-time, low-paying jobs, are all too common. Typically, women work as waitresses, bar girls, sales clerks, cooks, and so on. Older women often sell insurance, but they may also work as shop attendants or be employed by building maintenance firms to clean offices.

A 1987 study of 494 cases showed that slightly over 80 percent of divorces involved children younger than age twelve. In most cases, it was the mother who got custody, but more than half of these women received no child support.[13] Even in cases of mediated divorces only 67.2 percent required the father to pay child support, and even when agreement on child support was reached, not all the fathers met their obligations (only 13 percent in the above study).

It is only since around 1965 that child custody has been awarded more frequently to mothers than to fathers; in 1950, for example, in nearly half of the cases custody went to the father (in 11 percent, joint custody was awarded). In 1989, however, 71.3 percent of divorced mothers had custody of their children. The change reflects a shift in Japanese notions of the family, from that outlined in old, prewar civil codes (which almost always gave the head of household, the father, exclusive rights, including child custody) to a more individualistic approach. In the old days, both wife and children "belonged," as it were, to the family, and, while divorce allowed the wife to leave, the children stayed, most often to be raised by the paternal grandparents.

The Japanese fathers' apparent irresponsibility in child support may also reflect a traditional Japanese understanding of the family. While raising an heir, preferably male, is the reason that many Japanese get married and while many still strongly believe that divorce should be avoided for the sake of children, once a marriage is broken, the tie between the children and the noncustodial parent often is viewed as severed. Instead, the extended family of the custodial parent often steps in, feeling responsible. When my friend Sasaki Saeko divorced seven years ago, her parents took her and her daughter, then age six, into their modest house; in her neighborhood, she knew of other cases with similar arrangements. As Saeko did not have a regular job at that time, this was the only way for her and her daughter to survive.

Japanese society, now more accepting of divorce, assumes that neither women nor men are gravely disadvantaged by it. When one examines the lives of divorced mothers with minor children, however, this does not seem to be the case. A 1983 government survey, for example, showed that the income of a single-parent family headed by a mother was about half that of a two-parent family; among single-parent families, those headed by divorced mothers had a considerably lower income than those headed by widowed mothers.

Divorced mothers are disadvantaged in another way as well. For instance, under the government's child welfare provisions, divorced mothers are not entitled to any of the benefits that widowed mothers receive, such as interest-free educational loans and low-rent housing and pensions.[14] The inequities in the treatment of these two kinds of families thus reveal the government's discriminatory attitude toward divorced mothers. At least until recent years, Japanese businesses and industries seemed to approach divorce with a similar sentiment. While they have sometimes been sympathetic toward the families of deceased employees and might offer a widow a job, there has been no such consideration in cases of divorce.

A 1985 change in child allowance provisions for divorced mothers reflects this punitive attitude toward divorced women. With the rationale that increasing work opportunities were available for women, the government introduced a minimum income requirement for mothers who wished to receive welfare. Although this might be considered a realistic measure, reflecting the increasing earning power of women, the rule also states that the income of the noncustodial father must also be considered in determining a woman's eligibility. Since the government does little to ensure that fathers actually contribute support, the new regulation ignores reality and simply punishes divorced mothers. Some see this as a sign of collective pressure against further dissolutions of marriages involving children.

The plight of single fathers who raise children alone is receiving attention as such cases start to emerge. (The media have picked up this new social phenomenon and introduced it in television dramas as well as in documentary news reports.) Rather than financial problems, the difficulties in these cases seem to center on the fathers' adjustment to a seemingly impossible situation. The lack of discipline and of emotional support networks are reportedly more often problems for their children than for those living with mothers alone. It is apparent that the Japanese are now facing a new kind of social disintegration. As more children are affected by their parents' divorces, concern for divorce has taken on a whole new dimension.

4

Mothers' Children

During the post-World War II era, Japanese popular films and songs quite often depicted a mother who happily sacrifices herself for her family; she denies her sexuality and lives only for her children. Quite often fate has been unkind to her, and she is poor, with many struggles with life. Considering the real hardship the Japanese experienced during the postwar period, this representation has an element of truth. Mothers, many of whom were without their husbands, might indeed not have been able to manage a decent life for their families unless they denied their own desires. "Women are weak but mothers are strong," an expression popular in those days, described the situation, which lasted until the beginning of the 1960s.

The common perception of motherhood in the next decade can be seen in one of the most popular songs of the era, *Konnichiwa Akachan* ("Hello, My Baby"). This song about a young mother admiring her baby celebrates motherhood in a nontraditional nuclear family.[1] A time of rapid economic growth, the 1960s were also a time when the ideal of "my homism," or family centeredness, began to permeate urban middle-class families. The introduction of electrical appliances made work around the house easier, allowing mothers more free time to devote to their children, particularly to their education. Due to increasing Western influence, the English word "mama" began replacing the Japanese word, ōkasan. With husbands working harder than ever and away from home most of their waking hours, the psychological tie between mother and child was reinforced. A declining family fertility rate (1.54 in 1990 compared to 5.11 in 1926) strengthened this bond. This was the era when kyōiku mama (education moms) emerged.

One of the most popular songs of 1968, "Entrance Exam Blues," introduced "education moms" to the Japanese public as controlling, selfish women who lived their lives vicariously through their sons' academic achievement. The news media focused on the negative influence of these mothers upon their children and criticized them. According to sociologist Amano Masako, it was also around this time that Japanese mothers themselves began expressing a sense of loss of direction and of their lives being empty.[2] Considering my own mother, I find a relationship between her strong interest in her children's education and the fact that she found herself, in the early 1950s, with free time, relieved of time-consuming chores around the house. Among the forerunners of the "education moms," however, she appears not to have had a clearly defined goal or ambition for herself, which some people seem to associate with "education moms." She simply had energy and time to spare, and, as is the case with most Japanese mothers, her children were her first concern.

Rapid and large-scale industrial development and a mass exodus of people from villages and small towns during the 1950s and early 1960s resulted in the expansion of large industrial centers in Japan. This has presented new situations for mothers and their children. Although urbanization is a universal phenomenon of all industrial nations, the

Japanese version produced more drastic problems because of its speed, which was roughly four times that of the United States. In order to accommodate this large flow of people, major cities constructed enormous residential complexes on their outskirts. Unlike similarly constructed communities in other countries, such as Britain, these complexes—*nyū taun* ("new town") as the Japanese call them—consist exclusively of apartment houses. Since no shops or offices were built in conjunction with the apartments, these new towns are also called *beddo taun* ("bed town"), a place where people return to sleep. The distance of these homes from the city centers has produced many problems.

Extreme and rapid urbanization meant that most mothers were raising their children in an environment entirely different from the one in which they themselves had been raised; they lacked the social networks that had existed for their mothers. A new mother might be left with books on child rearing and a couple of phone numbers to connect her to the outside, to people who could understand her problems and give advice.

Studying popular articles from magazines and newspapers during the 1970s, Amano found that mothers were now portrayed as if they were merciless "ogres"; it was around this time that infanticide began receiving attention from reporters as a newly emerging social pathology.[3] A new type of child desertion began to be noticed around the same time; dead bodies were even found in such unheard-of places as coin lockers in train stations (in contrast to the backdoor of someone's house, as in the common practice of old days). Writing on this bizarre new form of child desertion, poet Kōra Rumiko composed a poem entitled "Koin rokā no kurayami" ("Darkness Inside the Coin Locker"); Sakamoto Ryū wrote a novel called *Koin rokā beibīzu* (*Coin Locker Babies*).

Because Japanese culture has traditionally emphasized the mother-child relationship and because people think that a mother "naturally" bonds with her child, rather than learning once she becomes a mother, cases of abusive mothers are seen as caused by a loss of basic human decency. This is evident in such a headline as "Maternal Instinct Gone Berserk" for an article reporting a case in which a mother killed her three-month-old baby so that she could go back to work and start saving money to buy a house.[4] What is missing in some of these reporters' views is that, in an age when family life has been dramatically altered, some young mothers are having a great deal of difficulty, and their frustration is shared by more mothers than one might think.[5]

One of my elderly woman acquaintances believes that a shift in the attitude toward procreation is related to many difficulties that Japanese mothers are facing today in raising children. In earlier times, children were simply born, but now they are "planned." Instead of perceiving children as future caretakers who will look after them in their old age, parents now produce offspring so that they can experience emotional satisfaction. My acquaintance claims that here is a source of Japanese parents' indulgence toward their children and their loss of control, resulting in various problems.

The life cycle of Japanese women has also changed, affecting the parent-child relationship. In 1940, the average number of years between a woman's marriage and the birth of her first child was three; by 1978, this interval had been reduced to thirteen months. The majority of women now have their first child during their first or second year of marriage, when they are barely adjusted to this major life change. Since a wide age gap between the first and second child is generally considered undesirable, mothers now have the second child at about age twenty-eight (in contrast to age thirty-five for their mothers, who did not mind spreading out their childbearing over a period of fifteen years).[6]

As noted, the physical environment in which many Japanese mothers raise their children has changed greatly from that of earlier times as well. In 1987, I lived with my family in a neighborhood of one of the new towns on the outskirts of Osaka. Throughout our nine-month stay, I witnessed continuous urban development around us. Next to a nearby bamboo forest, more apartment buildings were being built; adjacent to newly laid concrete roads were still a few farmhouses with thatched roofs and small rice paddies between them. The feeling of artificiality and the lack of continuity that characterized this neighborhood seemed eerie. A woman I befriended confided that she felt "a strange aversion" to the next-door neighbors on both sides of her apartment unit. The knowledge that her neighbors, literally thousands of them, lived in a space of exactly the same size and floor plan had a strange effect on her psyche, she said. Physical proximity seemed, ironically, to work against the residents of the new town becoming close to their neighbors; during the nearly ten years my acquaintance had lived there, she had not made any good friends. The aversion described is related to living without any meaningful human network in enclosed spaces that are identified, for instance, as "building Q, unit 711." By 1985, 77 percent of the entire Japanese population lived in urban areas, and three-quarters of the urban population lived in the three major metropolitan areas that have several new towns.

After talking with quite a few mothers during my stay in Japan in 1987, I concluded that Japanese mothers, particularly younger mothers, perceive child rearing as a difficult task. In conjunction with a lack of adequate living space and the high cost of education, this perceived difficulty is a reason for limiting the desired number of children to one or two.

Japanese mothers today complete their childbearing within a little over three years after marriage.[7] In terms of the mothers' extended life expectancy, the time spent on child rearing represents only a small portion of their lives. Even with the society's emphasis on motherhood, it is now much more difficult to be satisfied with simply being a mother, and many mothers are realizing this. For those who want to work outside the home, however, finding child care is the biggest hurdle. Not uncommon in many societies, this difficulty is even greater in Japan, where child-care centers, most of which are public facilities, have inflexible hours, where there is usually a long commute between home and work, and where fathers are either unwilling or unable to share responsibility.

Consider the situation of my friend Kusunose Mikiko. The mother of two children, ages four and two, Mikiko, who works at an advertising firm in central Tokyo, leaves home around 7:30; she drops her children at day care on her way to the station, arriving at work by 9:00. She cannot make it to the day-care center to collect the children before it closes at 6:00, so she has hired a woman to do this for her and to stay with the children until she gets home, which is around 8:00 at night. Her husband, a computer programer, cannot help because he leaves home even earlier than Mikiko and returns home around midnight. The cost of child care, including hiring the woman, is not small—almost half of Mikiko's salary.

My friend, however, is lucky because she has found a public day-care facility that can take both of her children. The availability of such day care, with relatively small fees and supervision by the municipal government, depends upon one's geographical location; in order to qualify for such day care, mothers often have to go through a lot of red tape. Furthermore, since these facilities close at 6:00 (partly in order to protect the women who work there, but also on the grounds that keeping children longer than eight hours is not desirable), they do not fully meet the needs of mothers who have full-time jobs like Mikiko's.

What about private day care? Kawashima Shizuyo, the author of a book entitled *Yami ni tadayou kodomotachi* (*Children Drifting in the Darkness*) found out the reality of one kind. At a *bebī hoteru*, or baby's hotel, children and infants may be kept until after midnight, sometimes overnight. Often situated inside a high-rise building on a neon-lit street, sandwiched between a bar and a mahjong parlor, *bebī hoteru* are called "hotels" because they offer round-the-clock care. Many who avail themselves of these "hotels" are bar hostesses; some places have contracts with nightclubs, which advertise the availability of child care when recruiting hostesses.

The number of baby hotels mushroomed throughout Japan during the 1970s, although most Japanese learned about their existence only through television news reports of various accidental deaths of the children in these hotels, mostly caused by suffocation. Reports on these accidents, the poor conditions (up to twenty children looked after by one or two adults), and the long hours the children were being kept there appalled viewers. The reporters pointed out that, despite Japan's Child Welfare Law (which makes it clear that the government, along with parents, has a responsibility to provide adequate care and protection), the government has permitted a private industry to fill a void by insisting on the view that institutional care is undesirable for the young child. Investigation followed the news reports, and regulations governing baby hotels were written. According to Kawashima, however, there seems to have been little improvement.

In 1987, I saw one of these baby hotels in downtown Osaka, located amid restaurants, bars, and nightclubs. The children's colorful drawings, pasted on the windows, looked incongruous against the bright neon, but, in an age when women's employment has increased and diversified, a facility like this, with its great flexibility, is naturally appealing. According to a 1980 study, about half of the mothers who used baby hotels worked in order to support themselves and their children.[8] In Kawashima's book are dozens of photos. One shows a young girl, wide awake on a top bunk bed, waiting for her mother to pick her up while all the other children sleep; another shows a sign reading "Mother for Rent."

Considering education the key to the production of highly skilled, well-disciplined workers who support a nation's economic growth, U.S. news media have repeatedly reported how well the Japanese educational system works. Reporters point out that, in international comparisons, Japanese students score high not only in fields that require rote memory, but in areas like science as well. Some observers conclude that Japanese students are well educated because they spend more days at school (sixty more days a year than American children). Others assume that the Japanese educational system works because Japanese society is more homogeneous, and uniformity in teaching is maintained. Uniformity, it is true, is achieved through the use of a limited number of textbooks approved by the Ministry of Education; the national government also exerts a great deal of influence on curriculum development.

Yet another view suggests that the key to Japanese success in education is the high regard the Japanese have for the profession of teaching. Although there has been a definite corrosion in this attitude in recent years, regard still exists to a great extent. Moreover, Japanese primary and secondary school teachers tend to see themselves as engaged in a process they refer to as "life guidance." I witnessed this "life guidance" firsthand, when I sent my two children to public school in Osaka in 1987. For instance, during school lunch (compulsory during the first six years of public school), the teacher made sure that students ate all of their food—the teaching of a good habit; at a parent-teacher conference, my third-grade daughter's teacher expressed interest in my disciplinary approach at home. Home visits by teachers are part of their job, so that they can understand their students in their family environments. In other words, teachers are concerned with their students both in and out of school, and they expect a great deal of parental participation.

All of this said, however, there is no doubt that a very important key to high academic performance among Japanese students lies in a fierce competition they undergo, willingly or unwillingly, and the efforts of mothers to support and encourage their children to be winners. It is true, as Edwin Reischauer has pointed out,[9] that the importance of preparing for the required entrance examinations (for both high school and university) helps explain the seriousness with which the Japanese approach education.

The case of Kumiko and her mother, a friend of mine, is typical of ninth-grade students in Japan. Never very studious and busy with her school band, Kumiko did not do too much entrance exam preparation until six months before she was to take the exams to enter a high school. Then she began to study very hard. Every day she studied for a few hours after school and again after dinner, until she went to bed at 10:00; she then got up at 3:30 the next morning to study some more. Since her alarm could not completely wake her up, she enlisted the help of her willing mother, who, after waking Kumiko, returned to bed. During the two weeks of winter break, Kumiko also went all day to a *juku*, a cram school. She told me that her classmates stopped talking about their favorite television programs as the entrance exam date approached and instead shared information on the test and how to solve difficult math problems.[10]

With its focus on helping children pass entrance examinations, the *juku* features motivational techniques and more advanced teaching than does regular school. During a 1983 visit to Japan, I discovered how widespread the practice of sending children to a *juku* had become. Cramming schools had become so popular, I was told, that those who did not attend one had problems finding playmates after regular school. Children now also start *juku* earlier, sometimes during the fourth grade. *Juku* are run by private enterprise and are costly; some mothers take a part-time job so that they can afford the expense.

In Japan today, it is considered the mother's responsibility to see that her children do well at school and are prepared to receive an optimal education. Hence, the mother encourages, scolds, bribes, and does anything else that might help her child study. Unlike American mothers, who tend to see their role in their child's achievement as limited, perhaps because they believe that the key component is the child's innate ability to learn, Japanese mothers emphasize effort as most important for success.[11]

I observed how far this effort to help their children succeed can go with an old friend, Toda Akiko. The mother of a fifth-grade boy at the time I visited her in 1987, Akiko told me of her educational plan for her son. The Todas live in Miyazaki, a remote town on Kyushu, where Akiko's husband teaches at a university, but Akiko has a plan to move to Tokyo with her son within a few years. She claims that the best high schools in the country are found only in a few big cities and that her husband, an unusually self-sufficient man for a Japanese husband, will not mind being left behind. Until then, during school breaks, Akiko has been accompanying her son on two-hour plane trips to Tokyo, so that he can attend one of the more prestigious *juku* there.

Akiko does not consider herself an "education mom," for the term has been used in the recent past to describe mothers who pressure their children—mostly sons—into unreasonable study habits. As the leader of a women's volunteer organization, she has other interests besides being a mother. In her calm description of the realities of competition in Japan's educational system, I did not detect any traces of the obsessiveness of an egocentric mother who lives her life vicariously through her son. Nonetheless, when we met to talk about old times, Akiko showed me a few geometry problems she had helped her fifth-grader with the night before. I could see then that preparing for the examination is not a task for a child alone. Clearly more is expected of Japanese children now than when Akiko and I were primary school students thirty-five years ago—or of the majority of American children of comparable age today.

I see another dimension to Japanese educational competition. The degree of sacrifice that Japanese parents are willing to make so that their children receive the best possible education can be understood more fully if education is seen clearly as an investment. If one asks Japanese parents what they consider the most important investment for the future, many will answer "children." In their minds, the child's (mainly the son's) secure financial future, with lifetime employment in a large and well-established firm, is equivalent to their own future security.

The same perspective is reflected in the parents' preferences for their children's future careers. Many parents want their sons to go into engineering (30 percent, in one study) and government work (19 percent), two of the most promising and secure fields.[12] Both because of the traditional emphasis on filial responsibility and because social welfare provisions in Japan have long been paltry and subject to the vicissitudes of the country's economy, many Japanese expect that their children—sons in most cases—will take care of them, if necessary, in their old age. Parental expectations for their children's future careers often differ according to the gender of the child, likewise manifesting the view of education as an investment.[13]

Education at pre-college levels has become quite expensive in Japan in the past few decades, due to the practice of sending students to *juku* and hiring private tutors, as well as to the increased popularity of private schools. The average annual cost of high school education (both public and private) in 1983, for instance, was as much as 210,000 yen ($1,680).[14] Many households put aside a good portion of their year-end bonuses (often equivalent to three months' salary) either to cover their children's educational expenses or to save for the future, instead of spending the money for pleasure and the enrichment of their present lives. This practice perhaps is related to the high level of personal savings among the Japanese. Couples have also been opting to have fewer children so that they can afford the "right" education for them.

Many Japanese are disturbed by what they consider to be excessive educational competition, accompanied by parents' pouring money into their children's education. Despite the criticism, however, the majority continue to feel that they have no choice. The villain, they say, is the *gakureki shakai*, or diploma-oriented society. The dramatic increase in interest in higher education, however, seems inevitable; it partially reflects changes in the Japanese economy—the very rapid shift from manufacturing to high-tech and other industries that require higher education. College education is more important now than even a decade ago. Thus, despite the rising cost of education at all levels, the desire of Japanese parents to provide their children with higher education has steadily increased. One poll has shown that as many as 79 percent of them want their sons (24 percent for daughters) to receive a four-year college education.[15] Although many new colleges have opened in the past few decades, this level of parental expectation is not matched by educational resources. Hence, high competition rates.

A mother who wants her child to succeed—as most do—will continue to sacrifice not only money but much personal time and effort to support the child's "examination years." A friend of mine, a professional woman, recently told me in a letter that she plans to cut back her hours of work to help her daughter pass her high school exams. I do not expect a lessening of this maternal fervor in Japanese mothers in the coming years.

5

Daughters: Young Women Today

During a short visit to Japan in the winter of 1989, I was introduced to a novel by a man named Murakami Haruki, entitled *Noruue no mori* (*Norwegian Woods*, 1987). It was extremely popular then, topping the best-seller list for more than a year. Basically a love story, it depicted some young men and women vividly. I felt that the novel represented new ways in which young Japanese today might think, feel, and relate to each other.

The novel's main character, Watanabe Tōru, is a college senior, living alone in a Tokyo apartment. He is a sensitive and likable person with refined taste; he nonetheless gives the distinctive impression of being a loner, unconnected to people, or to anything else around him, for that matter. His passivity and lack of a strong will to shape his future are apparent in more than a few ways.

The two main women presented in the novel, Midori and Naoko, could not be more different from each other, and yet, neither is a "traditional" Japanese woman. Midori is an outgoing college senior who knows what she wants and does not hesitate to go after it. Naoko, who seems equally different from her mother's generation in her opinions about sex, marriage, and family, has had a mental breakdown and is being treated in a sanitarium. Tōru visits Naoko there and tries to persuade her to leave the sanitarium to live with him; she refuses. More and more, Tōru lets himself become involved with Midori, who has been pursuing him, but, at the news of Naoko's suicide, he becomes emotionally paralyzed. The novel ends with the suggestion that Midori is no longer interested in Tōru when he finally pulls himself together.

Another example of a new attitude among young people is found in a novella by a young woman named Yoshimoto Banana, entitled *Kicchin* (*Kitchen*), which, when published in 1987, caused "Bananamania."[1] Yoshimoto's heroine, Sakurai Mikage, is also a lonely soul, who has just lost her only family, her grandmother. Other characters—Mikage's friend and his transsexual father who owns a gay bar—are also not types with which my generation was familiar. They are urbanites without traditional family ties, living in a small, cell-like, condominium unit.

Both Yoshimoto and Murakami, belong to the generation that grew up listening to the Beatles (reflected in the title of Murakami's novel) and taking a Westernized lifestyle and material affluence for granted. Both the authors and their characters belong to the generation labeled *shinjinrui*, or "new *Homo sapiens*." They are young men and women whose sensibility, taste, and philosophy are different from members of the generation that remembers childhood experiences of bombings and food shortages, who were single-mindedly involved in helping to make Japan the world's leading economic power.

To many older Japanese, the term *shinjinrui* denotes decadence and a reaction against traditional virtues of diligence, discipline, and delayed gratification. *Shinjinrui* are members of the generation who have grown up on new technology and a multitude of information sources, who consider work an unavoidable necessity, not a virtue. Instead of conformity, they value individuality, particularly in matters of personal taste. A Japan Broadcasting Corporation survey showed that only 25 percent of respondents in their twenties—in comparison with 54 percent of those in their fifties—were willing to sacrifice their private life partially for their company.[2] The same survey showed that *shinjinrui* are also politically conservative (males more so than females) and have a deep distrust of their government. They are unwilling to sacrifice personal time for public causes and tend to be uninterested in participating in legitimate social and political protest.

A finding in a 1988 survey by the Prime Minister's Office seemed to indicate that the elderly (those age sixty and over) felt a change in the value of young Japanese; more than a quarter of elderly women respondents (slightly less among male) felt that being old signified "inferior" to young people. This percentage, indicating a felt lack of respect, is nearly three times higher than among American, British, and French respondents.[3] This is contrary to the traditional notion (with which my generation was inspired) that the elderly deserve respect.

One distinctive characteristic of the *shinjinrui* characters created by Murakami and Yoshimoto is that they value casual relationships with others. Even their few essential relationships, although amiable, seem shallow; thus there is a prevailing sense of loneliness. This trait is related to their sense of belonging: they consume, for instance, in a manner that shows their membership in a group. Yamashita Etsuko, the author of *Sayonara Hanakozoku* (*Good-bye, Hanako Groupies*, 1992) thinks this is a serious problem. Young women today, according to Yamashita, enjoy ample opportunities and a degree of financial independence unknown to women of earlier generations, and they are also vocal in demanding more rights. They are, however, caught "in a labyrinth," as it were, and, being unable to handle the huge choices available, turn to media-created models found in magazines—*Hanako*, for example.[4] Author Yamashita believes that the obsession (she calls it a "syndrome") with a group orientation picked up from women's magazines is also seen in the workplace; many seem to choose jobs primarily for money and do not take responsibility at work seriously. They try hard to enjoy spending their income (many of them continue to live in their parents' houses without contributing their share and thus have even more money to spend) on various forms of leisure activities, including travel abroad.

I personally know a few *shinjinrui*, like Masako, the daughter of a hard-working journalist friend. The only child of a divorced couple (not all that rare with the increasing divorce rate among couples with children), Masako grew up managing her time on her own and having ample spending money. When in high school, she said that she hung out at coffee shops, snack bars, and discos in downtown Tokyo. Much of what Masako told me was surprising news to me, for when her mother and I were in high school, there was little opportunity for much diversion. Like an increasing number of young women, she opted to go abroad—ostensibly to study English, but actually to follow a popular trend and enjoy greater freedom rather than studying hard to get into Japanese college.

Shimojū Akiko published a book in 1976 based on interviews that she had conducted with women who were twenty-four years old (*Yureru nijūyonsai, Wavering Age, Twenty-Four*). A decade later, she repeated the interviews on a new group of women, again age twenty-four (published as *Nijūyonsai no kokoro moyō, Patterns of Women's Mind at Age Twenty-Four*). What came out of these two sets of interviews are the changes observed in young women's views and in their patterns of behavior today; these resemble those frequently mentioned above as characteristics of the *shinjinrui*. While many younger women now have more choices in many areas of their lives at work and play, and while some are taking advantage of the increased opportunities, others seem at a loss and unable to make decisions on their own. They appear to be "paralyzed" amidst plenty.[5]

Another author, Mizuno Mari, who looked into this phenomenon of paralysis among young women today in her book *Sekando bājin shindorom* (*Second Virgin Syndrome*), concluded that abundantly available information on sex, love, and relationships has resulted in enough confusion and uncertainty for some young women to avoid acting altogether. Despite their appearance of being independent-minded go-getters, says Mizuno, some are emotionally unable to make conscious decisions. The result is either seeking refuge in marriage (believing that it gives the answers to all the difficult questions) or remaining celibate. This analysis seems to fit Shimojū's observation that, to her surprise, several women she interviewed were still virgins at age twenty-four.

Tokyo rabu stōri (*Tokyo Love Story*) was a hit television drama series of 1991, based on a comic-book series of the same title. While the popularity of this series may have sent a message that it is acceptable for the woman to make the first step and ask for sex (as one of the two main characters does), it also seems to reveal the dichotomy between freedom of choice and the "emotional paralysis" of today's young women (and also young men) in the area of love and marriage.

Contrary to the popular perception that *Tokyo Love Story* is a story of *jun'ai*, or "pure-love," it is actually a listless tale of a young man and two women who cannot figure out how they feel, but who somehow reach an acknowledgment of one another's feelings at the end of the story. In the sense that action precedes feelings, romance among today's young Japanese in reality resembles traditional *miai* (without parental involvement), according to Satō Kenji.[6] Through analysis of *Tokyo Love Story* and other love comedies popular among young Japanese during the past decade, he has concluded that "make-believe" situations where partners are "only playing at love" represent Japanese youthful romance today.

The great love story popular among my generation as we were growing to young adulthood was a tragic drama in which lovers encountered various obstacles caused by a patriarchal system before being reunited. Machiko, the heroine in an immensely popular 1950s radio drama, *Kimi no na wa* ("Your name . . ."), over whose fate thousands of listeners once shed tears of sympathy, finally overcame her adversaries because of her pure love and determination. In *Tokyo Love Story*, the obstacles are inward—one woman cannot make up her mind about whom she loves (although she finally returns her affection to her original suitor) and the other, the go-getter, is fearful of the prospect of being tied down when the man she pursues falls for her. Love is no longer an act of defiance against authority figures, and love stories have become tales of "love paralysis." Since the lovers can be brought together at last only by sheer chance, their stories are destined to be comedies. Although Satō and others seem to emphasize that this is a uniquely Japanese phenomenon, the inability to love and the escape into fantasy seem to be shared by American counterparts as well.

Some historical background on the leisure-time activities of the Japanese in the last three decades may be helpful to give a framework for the pattern of today's young people's behaviors and lifestyles. Among many other conspicuous changes in the lives of the Japanese people in the 1960s was an increase in leisure time. Free time was no longer merely rest from the labor necessary for livelihood. The word *rejā* (from the English "leisure") first appeared in the news media and in people's conversations around 1961; it reflected the fact that the Japanese, particularly young people, had begun actively enjoying free time. How to spend disposable income also became important.

About the same time, household appliances became readily available, and instant, precooked, and frozen foods were introduced into daily life. The new variety of food products gave the Japanese the opportunity to consume complexly. Ramen noodles, for example, first offered to the ever-busier consumer in 1958, were soon to be manufactured by 300 different companies. The proliferation of U.S. fast-food chains, such as McDonald's and Kentucky Fried Chicken, which occurred during the early 1970s, derived from the new popularity among the Japanese for eating out. As more people bought cars for leisure activities, more families, as well as young men and women, ate at restaurants. With their parking lots and reasonable prices, these restaurants helped alter the Japanese lifestyle. Spending on dining out steadily increased, as did expenditures for other recreational activities.

Patterns of alcohol consumption also underwent changes. In the postwar era, people usually drank in shabby, makeshift bars or small stalls, where wine made from sweet potatoes was served; the customers were exclusively men who sought a moment of relaxation on their way home from work. Around the 1960s, some conspicuous changes started to show, and on the streets of Ginza in Tokyo, for example, the small bars run by individuals, often by women, began to be replaced by those owned by corporations.[7]

By the mid-1970s, health workers had begun noticing that an increasing number of women were becoming dependent on alcohol, and astute television viewers observed that more women were portrayed drinking both in commercials and in dramas. It was no longer rare to see women in bars, either by themselves or in the company of men. Journalist Takada Masatoshi has claimed that it was mainly young women who instigated the change.[8] A concerted effort by the alcoholic beverage industry, which targeted women and their growing disposable income and greater freedom, was a contributing factor. Today, going to cafe-bars and having cocktails, supposedly to stimulate witty conversation, is a trendy activity for young men and women. Readers of novels by Murakami and Yoshimoto notice that their young female characters treat alcohol quite casually and sometimes drink heavily—an astonishing phenomenon for my generation, for whom women's drinking was limited to those in the "water trade" (that is, women who work in bars and other similar establishments).

College students in Japan enjoy ample leisure time and disposable income. According to a survey conducted by two Tokyo universities (private coeducational schools), students, especially female students, seem greatly interested in how to enjoy college life. Areas where they look for pleasure are music, cars, and fashion. Preparation for employment and education and training in special fields ranked next in their interests.[9] College students in my time as well as subsequent baby boomers (those born between 1947 and 1950, who are sometimes called *kyūjinrui*, or "the old *Homo sapiens*") wanted to be seen as rebellious, argumentative, and knowledgeable; college students nowadays place a higher value on being sincere, good-natured, likable, and gentle.

Student life in my era was synonymous with frugality. A ten-foot-square room at my dormitory was shared by two, sometimes, three, students, with no space other than for beds and desks. The off-campus apartment a friend had in her senior year was twice as spacious, but it was a room in her landlord's house, with shared entrance, bathroom, and hallway. Honjō Minako, the daughter of my college friend and now a sophomore at the Tokyo Science University, in contrast, has a room in a ten-story women's dormitory equipped with an electronic lock system, a laundry room, and a luxurious common lounge. In her room, Minako has many things her mother did not have: a television set, compact disc player, videocassette recorder, and an answering machine. Her rent is 82,000 yen ($650) a month, close to ten times what her mother paid thirty years ago. According to an informal survey conducted in 1989 by Shitamori Masumi, the monthly expenses of private university students in Tokyo and its vicinity averaged around 200,000 yen ($1,600) a month, not including tuition.[10]

Although many college students receive their living expenses from their parents (according to a 1988 survey by the Tokyo Federation of University Cooperatives, the average Tokyo student receives 115,000 yen or about $920 a month), many also work tutoring high school students, teaching at cram schools, and doing other types of part-time work. Minako's friend makes 8,000 yen a day being a "companion girl" who demonstrates products at trade fairs; as a dependent of her parents, she can earn up to 900,000 yen ($7,200) a year tax free.

The college students' focus on having a good time, rather than studying, is often explained as recovery from the long years of strenuous preparation for entrance examinations. Skipping class, particularly by those who major in the liberal arts and social sciences, is widely practiced. Female students typically enjoy such activities as going to town, window shopping, eating out, and having coffee with friends. *Kurabu* (clubs) of all sorts—sports, arts, English conversation, even *ren'ai kurabu*, in which members discuss "relationships" and conduct mutual guidance—are very important parts of their days. The *kompa* (from "companionship"), a get-together of students from different campuses, is also very popular; here, as well as at various campus festivals, members of the opposite sex meet one another. Masako told me that these activities are for fun, not for husband-hunting. As noted in Chapter 1, few female college students marry their college boyfriends.

Among the crowd of well-wishers gathered at the gate of the Imperial Palace at the end of 1989, when the late Emperor Hirohito was terminally ill, were some teenage girls in their school uniforms. Ōtsuka Eiji, a free-lance writer, wondered why they were there. These girls were not likely to have an ideological or political reason to show an interest in the welfare of Emperor Hirohito. Eventually, Ōtsuka concluded that the girls were drawn to the palace gates by their private image of the emperor—an image of loneliness, fragility, and unworldliness, a "rarified version of a kind of insulated existence."[11] Some of the girls referred to the emperor as "kind of sweet," a perception radically different from that of older generations. The quality to which these teenage girls responded may be called "ethereal."

Around the time of the late emperor's terminal illness, a young pop singer, Okada Yukiko, committed suicide prompting a mini-epidemic of teen suicides. These events together offer insight into the psychological framework of today's teenage girls in Japan, according to Ōtsuka. Okada's suicide notes disclosed that she was living in a fantasy world that she had invented in order to shield herself from the outside world. Few things seem to provoke stronger responses from today's Japanese teenage girls than images of sweetness and fragility. They yearn for an insulated world, a place of refuge from the crassness and ruthlessness of daily life.

Today's teenagers are the children of the baby boomers. Sometimes referred to as *ichigozoku* (the term was coined in the mid-1980s, meaning "strawberry group," but it is also a play on words: ichi=one, go=five, or fifteen, their average age), they are roughly the equivalent of America's Generation X (born between 1961 and 1981). Hirai Mamoru, a producer of Nippon Cultural Broadcasting, has discovered that the strawberry kids are hard to read. They possess high buying power, but it is impossible to predict their taste. Although they seem to be overwhelmed by psychological and physical changes, they find it difficult to talk to others about them; they are also less willing to be involved in others' affairs than older generations.[12]

I have a friend who lives in a newly developed luxury suburb outside of Yokohama. The suburb features "Dogwood Plaza" (dogwoods were first brought to Japan as a present from the U.S. government in return for the cherry trees now found along the Potomac River in Washington, D.C.), which is filled with cute and trendy shops interspersed with American fast-food chains and cake-and-coffee shops. According to my friend, this is where the new breed of teenage girls can be seen. Mostly from well-to-do families, they are used to a luxury we had never seen during our days, and they seem to be completely free from assigning special value to things from foreign countries as we did. American goods to them are simply "cute." They are more likely than those of earlier generations to be the only child of their parents (in 1989, households with one child under age eighteen stood at 37 percent), and so parents can lavish cash on their material needs. (In 1988, Japan's gross national product was the highest in the world, at about $23,300 per capita.) They seem to be free of the psychological barriers against other cultures held by older generations.

They also read comics about gender-role reversals. *Ranma 1/2* (*Ranma One-Half*) is a series of comics, referred to as *shōjo man'ga*, or girls' comics, although its readers, like my own teenage son, are not limited to girls. The central character, Ranma, is androgynous: Really a boy, he becomes a girl but returns to his original self by wetting himself with warm water. Akane, the female character, is quite a tomboy. The series recounts the various adventures in which these two are involved, tracing the mutual attachment and frustration between these two teenagers whose sexuality is unclear. In a similar type of comic popular in earlier days, androgyny had also been treated as the central theme. *Orufeusu no mado* (*Orpheus' Window*), published in the 1970s and perhaps one of the progenitors of this genre, is a story of romance and adventure against the background of the French Revolution.

Here, the central character is a girl who is beautiful, rich, and free to act as a boy.

These comics are stories of fantasy; in addition to themes of homosexuality, bisexuality, and transvestism, they explore aesthetics and decadence. In this world beyond-the-looking-glass, teenage girl readers seem to enjoy a freedom from the pressures of real life. Even in the comics more firmly grounded in reality, the denial of commonly observed practices is evident. In *Haikara-san* (*Miss High-Fashion*), for example, one sees a reverse situation of traditional patterns; here a gentle, caring father has a high-strung and aggressive daughter. The central character, Benio (a name that sounds like a boy's rather than a girl's), is skillful in *kendō* swordsmanship; she likes to drink, too, and is determined to choose a lover and job on her own.

The world of girls' comics has been enormously popular in recent years,[13] and many of them have been dramatized in television series. Here one can sense the strawberry generation's propensity to imagine freely and also its longing to escape. When I was their age, all we had available was classical Western fairy tales, with a Prince Charming and a princess perpetually waiting for a miracle, or Japanese folktales that attempted to teach feminine obedience and perseverance.

My daughter, who is sixteen years old, names *Heathers* as one of her favorite movies, and she has seen it numerous times. Obviously having strong appeal for her generation, the movie is filled with violence—attempts at murdering football players, mass suicide, and blowing up a school building—and with pointed comments on the smugness of main characters' parents' generation, the baby boomers. The members of Generation X represented in this movie (and most of its viewers) are kids "growing up too tough to be cute, . . . more comfortable shopping or playing than working or studying."[14] This American generation was raised in a country experiencing social changes; a sharp rise in single-parent households because of divorce; the widespread latch-key phenomenon among children; and an absence of heroes. These young people feel, as my daughter says, trapped and scared, but, out of necessity, they have learned a street-sense pragmatism. They have also learned to be cynical about adults whom they perceive to be "sensitive yet powerless." Perhaps these are characteristics more common in this age group than specifically American. I find similar traits in Japan's strawberry generation. Japan has its share of teenagers who act out their anger, mistrust, and frustration in delinquent or antisocial behavior. Although relatively small, the number of so-called *hikōshōjo*, or delinquent girls, described below, has been steadily increasing since the beginning of the 1980s. (Because of the lack of studies on female teenage delinquency, journalistic accounts are the best source of information.)

One girl's story, told in a book entitled *Hikōshōjo to yobu maeni* (*Before You Call Them Delinquent Girls*), by Hayashi Masayuki (1981), is that of Kanako. Kanako began smoking the year she entered an all-girls private high school. When someone saw her puffing away with several others behind the school building and reported her, Kanako hit the informer several times. This retaliation was discovered, and the school punished Kanako with a one-week home detention. When she returned to school after the long week, she felt sincerely sorry for what she had done, but classmates avoided her, circulating and exaggerating her crime. Kanako did not return home that day; the following day, she went to school with her hair bleached reddish brown, confirming the opinion that she was indeed a *hikōshōjo*. She spent a great deal of time hanging out at game centers and loitering around shopping arcades; she also frequented *sunakku* (snack bars that serve alcohol along with light meals) and eventually ended up working at one of them. Popular among the regular customers, she soon started drinking and began having casual sex.

Delinquency can also involve sniffing paint thinner and taking drugs, and the age at which these behaviors start has been dropping steadily. For fourteen-year-old Yuri (described in the same book as above), curiosity was the motive behind sniffing paint thinner. Although she liked her teachers and her parents were reasonable people, Yuri felt "frustrated, stressed out" at times. Upon the suggestion of a friend she met at a disco, Yuri sniffed paint thinner until she began hallucinating; she eventually needed treatment for a serious gastrointestinal disorder.

During the 1970s, when sniffing paint thinner and glue became popular, over 15,000 school-age children were estimated to have experimented with these substances; some of these children have since experienced impaired motor and language functions. Between 80 and 120 accidental deaths (due to suffocation, as plastic bags are used to enhance the effect) occurred. The number of sniffers has steadily increased since, reaching 4 million in 1987. While the abuse among boys has remained constant, that among girls has shown a sharp increase, making up 26 percent of all teenage abusers.[15]

Kakuseizai, which literally means "stimulants," is sometimes the next step for teenage girls who have sniffed paint thinner. Stimulants are smuggled into Japan mainly by organized crime, and girls who want stronger substances can be easily tempted into using these drugs and, eventually, lured into prostitution. As part of a world-wide trend, drug trafficking in Japan has increased in recent years, after stricter penalties had temporarily reduced the number of offenders.[16] About half of the drug-related arrests made in 1980 involved members of organized crime, but about 20 percent of the remainder were teenagers, mainly girls.[17] Today, the treatment of girls in juvenile detention centers includes drug rehabilitation.

Teenage prostitution is a frequent topic of men's weeklies, such as *Pureibōi* (*Playboy*), and of late-night television shows.

According to reports by the National Police Headquarters, the number of girls under age eighteen who were engaged in prostitution started to climb around 1974. Two years later, the number had quadrupled, and, by 1984, the number of teenage girls taken into police custody had reached 10,000. Almost all of these girls had become involved in prostitution willingly, often under the influence of friends. When free-lance reporter Fukiage Ryūichirō started investigating teenage prostitution, he had the preconception that it was extremely rare. He was wrong, and the following cases supply some details.[18]

Asako, age sixteen and a public high school student, lost her father when she was ten. In exchange for weekly sex with a man whom she called "Daddy," Asako received 50,000 yen ($370) a month, ten times her allowance. As this was not enough for her, she also went to hotels with various men she picked up on the street. Asako spent her money lavishly, treating her friends to movies and dinners.

Mikako, also sixteen, was from an ordinary middle-class family, with a father who was a company employee and a mother who was a part-time store clerk. She picked up her clients on her way home from school—in front of the train station, where, dressed in her school uniform, Mikako pretended to be waiting for her bus. As she reported, she rarely had to wait more than half an hour before a man would call out from his car and ask her to go for a drive. Several trips to a hotel resulted in as much as around 140,000 yen ($1,120) a month, money she spent on her boyfriend.

Kimiko's mother was divorced, and she supported her daughter by running a bar. When the bar was busy, Kimiko helped, and she soon developed seven or eight steady clients and an income of 50,000 to 200,000 yen ($370-$1,480) a month. She had two abortions, and, since she had to study to go to a college, she did not plan to increase her clientele.

The chief motivation for prostitution for these girls is to earn spending money. It can also be a game, however, as in the case of "group prostitution" that took place in Kōfu, Yamanashi Prefecture.[19] The situation began with two high school girls who worked at a department store cafeteria; the idea of prostitution was introduced by a bartender they befriended. Several of their friends were persuaded to join, and soon others started to work as prostitutes as the word spread. The girls were seen near their school and at the city center hunting for men with fancy cars. Police eventually found out about the situation by closely watching several motels, resulting in 100 girls being taken into custody. All from middle-class families, the girls had gotten involved in prostitution, not for the money, but for the treat of a single dinner and a thrill.

Teenage girls can also become involved in prostitution because of peer pressure or as a way to rebel. Fuyuko, whose story I read in a woman's magazine's "true story" column, stated as her motivation a general discontent. From a materially comfortable and reasonably harmonious family, Fuyuko described her father, a section chief in a mid-size firm, as a good provider but a hypocrite—an autocrat at home who could not be assertive at work; she was disgusted with him. Fuyuko was unhappy at school, which ranked its students rigidly according only to the results of tests. She was not a virgin when she engaged in prostitition for the first time.

According to the testimony of a gangster,[20] it is easy to spot potential teenage prostitutes in shopping centers, coffee houses, and discos. One simply behaves like a gentleman and asks a girl spotted if she would like to go somewhere for a nice dinner. Quite often she agrees, knowing what is going on, the gangster stated.

Contrary to popular belief, in other words, many teenage girls are neither forced nor deceived into prostitution. They may be lured by the idea of getting things they like—an expensive meal, special cosmetic products, or nice clothes. But, as Fuyuko testified, there can also be other factors. One sixteen-year-old girl, the daughter of a hard-working bureaucrat father and a full-time homemaker mother, reported that she was happy being recruited by a gangster because he was kind, generous, and, most importantly, honest with himself. By contrast, her father and teachers, who were concerned with others' opinions of them, appeared to live lives that were "circumscribed and empty."[21]

Many blame a proliferating sex industry for its exploitation of teenage girls; others feel that the girls' conduct is directly related to the increasingly hedonistic lifestyle of adults and to deteriorating family environments. Since 1956, any prostitution has been illegal in Japan, but men who pay to have sex with minors, with a few exceptions, are fined only a small amount of money if caught; the girls, on the other hand, are immediately expelled from school. The girls in Kōfu, described above, are said to have protested, when taken into police custody, that they had not done anything wrong. As long as one does not infringe on others' rights, they insisted, one can act according to one's wishes. Why was sex acceptable for adults but not for them, and why should they not try to get the money through the easiest way they know? The parents of these girls, by and large, remained ignorant of their daughters' clandestine activities. It would have astonished them to know that some of their daughters' made sure their customers could pay before they took off their clothes, and that they always carried "Mr. Kondo" (the Japanese slang for condoms). Reporter Fukiage found that some of the girls put money aside for a future abortion and that a primary concern was how to locate a "good" gynecologist.

Satō Etsuko of Rikkyō University has observed that patterns of prostitution eloquently tell, albeit in an exaggerated way, the sexual morality of a time. The illustrations given above reveal a situation in which prostitution is practiced by increasingly younger women. Another characteristic that was not seen three decades ago is its practice by a wide range of women—actresses, office workers, and even college students. As a result, the image of sleazy women in this line of work is being erased; this blurring of the barrier between "professionals" and part-timers has encouraged changes in the perception of prostitution. And these women are now found in various types of establishments, both old and new, which are generally referred to as *pinku sangyō*, sex (or pink) industry.[22]

Kabukicho in Shinjuku, Tokyo, is Japan's foremost night-life district, with gaudy neon lights and nonstop bustle. A tiny 0.34-square-kilometer zone, it is packed with bars, nightclubs, peep shows, *deito kurabu* (date clubs), *rabu hoteur* (lovers' hotels), and *sōpurando* (soaplands or massage parlors, which use to be called "Turkish baths" until official protests were made by the Turkish government due to the common association of the baths with prostitution).[23] Discos, whose chief clientele consists of teenagers, are also found here. This is where a veteran counselor, Kanematsu Sachiko, has been seeing various prostitutes since 1956, when an anti-prostitution law was enacted.[24] The majority of the women whom Kanematsu counseled when she started her job came from poor farming and fishing villages, and they worked as prostitutes in order to support their parents and siblings. Although women are no longer expected to sell themselves to help their families, according to Kanematsu, prostitution is more rampant in Shinjuku now; it has also become increasingly diversified.

Blatant advertising, in the form of flyers and stickers in public places (on telephone booths and lampposts), and the proliferation of pornography in weekly magazines and sports papers has had a numbing effect upon many Japanese, inviting poor resistance, if not tacit approval, of sex businesses. The signs of numbness can also be seen in the attitudes among young "part-time" prostitutes, as in the following cases that I found in a woman's magazine article, entitled "Why O. L. (Office Ladies) Prostitutes Are Popular?"[25]

A woman named Ayako dialed the number given in an advertisement for a "lovers' bank"; rebelling against her parents, who had chosen a husband for her, she was looking for adventure. After refusing the first prospective "date" referred to her, she found a client who gave her 200,000 yen ($1,480) a month for occasionally sleeping with him; she also went out to dinner and joined him on weekend trips. She had a boyfriend in addition to her approved fiancé, and, while she saved up money for her marriage, she planned to continue this job.

Minako, who is dating a forty-eight-year-old business owner, is less rebellious in her reasons for being a call girl. She likes her customer because he is worldly and takes her to expensive restaurants; he is also willing to listen when she needs to talk. A college student, Minako receives an allowance from her parents, which she puts into her savings account; the money given by her "date," however, she spends on travel with friends, including her boyfriend. She reasons that one should do many things while young. Nonetheless, with significant numbers of women in rehabilitation centers for prostitutes being emotionally unstable, having a history of psychological problems, or suffering from some type of handicap, counselor Kanematsu has maintained that the "uninformed, unformed sexual morality" of such women bears detailed scrutiny.

I have come upon one newspaper article that considered how young women with a good education might still be naive enough to be tricked and become involved in prostitution. Under the headline "Young Women Fell for 'First Class' and 'Prominent Men,'" *Kōbe Shimbun* (31 May 1985) reported the arrest of a brother-and-sister team for their prostitution scam. Of the 200 women who applied to a newspaper ad for "the job you can be proud of," only one-quarter passed the two interviews to be "partners to only well-known elite gentlemen." More than half of the women were college students and office workers. The key was a sleek sales pitch that boosted their egos ("you're high class, also"). By the time they had gone through "training" (on manners, makeup, even how to talk graciously), the article stated, none of the women withdrew, even when they became aware of the nature of their job. After all, it paid 80,000 yen ($400) for two hours; 320,000 yen ($1,600) for an overnight. While some participants agreed to write a pornography-like "report" on various clients, others were said to have commented that they "had a good time."

More often than not, however, women engaged in prostitution have complex reasons. Almost always, a poor self-image and sexual valuation are key factors. Satō's study showed that women involved in prostitution recognized it as "shameful." But, unlike guilt, shame is not felt as long as it is kept to oneself; the young women's naiveté might thus keep them unharmed so long as they can rationalize their behavior. Meanwhile, men who have prostitutes sent to their hotel rooms dispatch-style because it is a less threatening alternative to buying prostitutes at soapland can be open about it, but women almost always keep their involvement a close secret. Women's groups as well as educators and parents have become more active in recent years both in reexamining the Anti-Prostitution Law implemented and in eliminating various practices that perpetuate sexual inequality.

Acceptance of their society's double standard regarding sex is evident among Japan's young people in several ways. For example, there are two words in Japanese for virgin: *shojo* (for female) and *dōtei* (for male); while *shojo* is considered positive, *dōtei* implies an undesirable situation. "It's more natural for boys to want to have sex" is a readily accepted myth. The double standard was apparent also in a 1985 Lower House debate, in which a legal restriction on pornographic publications was proposed. While the Diet members—almost all male—objected that young women have access to sexual information and related material, they found other articles, such as "How to catch boys" and "How to please your boyfriend," in the same publication to be harmless.

Junketsu kyōiku (literally, "purity education") is another Japanese term reflecting the double standard. Meaning sex education, it implies that the main reason for teaching about sex is in order to condemn it outside the sanctified realm of marriage. Although this term has been officially replaced by the more straightforward term *sei kyōiku*, or sex education, the topic in the school curriculum has been, until very recently, limited largely to talking about the physical changes accompanying puberty. Surveys show that sex education at home is even poorer. The majority of Japanese parents and teachers still do not feel comfortable teaching about sex and are puzzled as to how they should approach the subject.[26]

That teenage sex cannot continue to be poorly dealt with was demonstrated in a 1981 survey conducted by *Poppu Tīn* (*Pop-Teens*), a monthly magazine for teenage girls. More than two-thirds of the respondents in this survey said that they were not virgins, and two-thirds of them had had their first intercourse at age fifteen or sixteen. Contrary to common notions, the survey also found that most of these girls had participated in sex willingly, rather than being forced. That teenage girls are sexually innocent is "a myth created by men," a sixteen-year-old girl respondent commented.[27]

Many teenagers today reportedly agree that sex is permissible if there is love; many more would agree if other conditions also exist: that one does not hurt others and that contraception is used.[28] Yet, according to the same survey, fewer than half of the high school seniors among the respondents used contraception at first intercourse. Although Japan's total number of abortions has declined in recent years, abortion among teenage girls has risen, and, when the Japanese Association of Obstetrics studied 857 pregnant teens in 1979, 23 percent of these unmarried teens had had at least one previous pregnancy. In another study, conducted in 1983, the number of abortions among teens was nearly 26,000, with a rate of 6.1 per 1,000 teenage girls. A 1985 survey on teens' opinions of abortion showed that close to half of high school seniors (slightly more girls than boys) approved of abortion if a pregnancy is unwanted.[29]

In the absence of adequate sex education, many Japanese teens obtain their knowledge of intercourse, contraception, and other matters from magazines, books, and friends. In 1986, according to Satō Etsuko, there were more than ten magazines for teenagers that published various articles related to sex, and a popular one regularly sold 200,000 to 300,000 copies.[30] Teenagers buy these magazines, full of graphic descriptions and *taikenki* ("My experience") pieces, and they secretly circulate them among friends at school. Some publications, referred to as *binīru bon* ("plastic-covered book") are sealed in clear plastic wrapping so that they cannot be read in the store; these are available at bookstores and from vending machines.

Information on commercialized sex and other sexually explicit material proliferate in any of Japan's large cities. While large movie posters showing near-naked women are in blatant display on busy downtown streets, it is common to see, on commuter trains, both young and middle-aged men reading sports newspapers with large photos of sexually explicit and often violent acts.[31] Many teenagers, even children who attend cram school, use these commuter trains and are exposed to this material daily. A thirteen-year-old boy who sometimes stops at a noodle shop on his way home from school told me that he finds magazines there with "a lot of interesting stuff—about soaplands, and things like that"—and that when he finds "particularly good ones," he tells his friends to go and look for themselves. When the Minors' Department of the Kanagawa Prefectural Police Headquarters investigated 2,000 randomly chosen vending machines that sold pornographic publications, it discovered that 30 out of 169 customers were high school students.[32]

Just how lucrative the marketing of these books is was illustrated by the testimony of a man who made 9 million yen ($600,000) in three months selling them through vending machines.[33] Funahashi Kuniko, a feminist scholar, maintains that women and teenage girls in today's Japan receive the message, through various forms of exposure, that they are to be sexually exploited and that men are animals destined to take advantage of female sexuality.[34] While they have been interested in the issue of pornography for some time now, Japanese feminists have recently become more active in educating women about the prevalent problem of sexual harassment in the workplace, another area of sexual concern.

6

Women and Work

In 1962, when I graduated from Tsuda College, most members of my graduating class who wanted to work had little trouble finding jobs. This was partly because Japan was in the middle of an economic boom but also because there were not many women with college degrees. With few exceptions, however, we did not consider our work a long-term career commitment. We assumed that we would leave our jobs upon marriage and that our husbands would support us. It was a time when the word *tomo-kasegi*, or dual-income couple, had a distinctly negative connotation. It meant that the husband did not make enough to support his family.

Of the four women who worked with me in publishing a campus literary magazine, only one had clear professional goals. She wanted to become an editor. Although very few women were in publishing at the time, she found a position in the publishing division of the Japan Travel Bureau. She eventually became a top editor and has been in the field for over thirty years now. She remained single—not because she was opposed to marriage, but because she felt it was impossible for her to have both a career and a family.

A second woman in our group also worked as an editor for a small food and nutrition magazine for a few years before going to graduate school to study linguistics. While in school, she married, and, when her husband's job made it necessary for him to leave Tokyo, she discontinued her studies. They eventually moved back to Tokyo, but returning to school was all but impossible for my friend. She became a part-time secretary to her husband, who had started a private legal practice. A third group member followed a similar course. While in graduate school at the prestigious University of Tokyo, she met her future husband. Later she found a part-time teaching position at a small all-girls college in the city to which she followed her scholar husband.

The fourth woman chose a more typical route for a Tsuda College graduate, becoming a high school English teacher in her hometown and quitting her job altogether when she got married. Life was going smoothly until her husband died suddenly in his early forties. In order to support herself and her two children, she returned to teaching at a private high school. She says she was lucky, for with the rigid employment practices in Japan at that time, it was extremely difficult to find a full-time teaching job after the age of thirty. She now works ten hours a day, which includes a long commute.

Without much thought, I chose to seek a job in advertising, then a newly developing field. Following common Japanese employment practices, I took an entrance exam for my job a few months before graduation; the exam consisted of written tests on Japanese and English skills and writing an essay. During the subsequent interview, I was given the impression that this firm was different from a typical Japanese business that gives its women employees subservient roles and tedious clerical chores. It was obvious during my first days of work, however, that no such difference existed. I evidently had little idea of how to plan or pursue a career. The following year, I went to the United States to study social work. After I received a graduate degree from the University of Denver, I returned to Japan at the end of 1965 and worked in a small mental health clinic and a newly established large-scale rehabilitation facility until another opportunity to live and work in the United States arrived. Frustration with the bureaucracy I had to deal with in my work made it easy for me to leave Japan for good.

Women in Japan have always worked. In 1955, for example, more than 50 percent of women did, albeit mainly in farming, fishing, and family-owned businesses.[1] Although "employment" in the modern sense of the word did not apply to these women, they worked long hours alongside men, in addition to raising several children and performing all the chores around the house. Some think that today's "workaholic" Japanese businessmen learned their work ethic from their hard-working mothers.[2]

This situation remained basically unchanged until the mid-1950s. During the next decade, farming rapidly declined, and men went to work in factories and other places, leaving their wives at home. As a result, the percentage of women engaged in some kind of paid work was lower during the 1970s, causing Japanese women to lose their status as workers. Although it picked up later, the total number of working women at the end of the 1980s had not quite reached the level of the 1940s.

Since 1969, the year that I left Japan for the second time, the employment picture for Japanese women has undergone a slow but substantial transformation. The number of women with full-time jobs has risen (more than doubled in twenty years); while only slightly more than 9 million women were wage earners in 1965, by 1990, more than 18 million women were employed, substantially more than the population increase. Women now constitute almost 40 percent of the work force; nearly 70 percent of these are (or have been) married. The increase has paralleled the change in the number of female college graduates, which nearly tripled between 1960 and 1975. By 1980, about one-third of all female high school graduates continued on to four- or two-year colleges, a sharp increase from the 5.5 percent who did so in the year I graduated.[3]

Until recently, women employees in Japan were usually young and unmarried. The term *koshikake shūshoku*, meaning temporary employment, applied to female workers who would leave a job after a few years to get married; many of them worked only up to their mid-twenties. In recent years, however, increasing numbers have chosen to continue working after marriage, even after having children. In fact, the number of these women has more than doubled in the past twenty years; in 1965 as many as 49 percent of new mothers quit work, but the figure had dropped to 24 percent by the end of the 1980s.[4] By the end of the 1980s, there were approximately 4 million women (or 27 percent of all working women) who had been steadily employed in the same place for ten years or more.

A fixed pattern of hiring, for both men and women, has long been practiced by Japanese employers, particularly by larger companies. New potential recruits almost always follow this pattern to find jobs as I myself did. First, a public announcement of openings for new employees is made in the fall, just once a year, in the middle of the Japanese school year. College (or high school) seniors then take written exams to be tested in both specific fields and in general knowledge. Recruiters then interview prospective employees.

Interviews for college women can still be a harrowing process, as was true for Michi, an acquaintance of mine who tried to get a job at a brokerage firm in 1987. "Are both your parents still alive?" was the first question she was asked. Five minutes into the interview, Michi reported, the manager continued to ask her about her family; he asked nothing about the political science courses taken at college, nor about other subjects pertinent to the job. Another woman who applied for a job at a trading firm was not even granted an interview. When she inquired about the reason, the personnel officer told her they could not consider her because the company did not have a women's dormitory. If a woman lives alone, away from her parents, this woman observed, her morality is called into question. Questions about parents and family indicate how some Japanese recruiters still approach women's employment. The implication of these questions is that a young woman would make a better and more stable employee if she lived in a traditional family unit. The same questions would never be asked of male recruits. The bias may reflect the fact that recruiters are mostly men. "Recruiting officers who visited our campus said they were eager to put women to work," Michi said, but when she visited the companies, none of them had a woman involved in the hiring process. "They were shuffling papers and serving tea."

Despite progress made in more recent years, most (though not all) Japanese business and industry have been reluctant to hire female graduates of four-year colleges. The argument has been that women recruited at age twenty-one or twenty-two quit too soon, in three or four years, in order to get married. Although an increasing number of women do not fit this pattern, employers, particularly those at large and more established firms, continue to believe that women differ from men in their motivation to work and that, for the kinds of work they expect women to perform, those with two-year college degrees are preferable.[5]

Although the perception has been slowly changing, it still is clear that, in employers' minds, there are different reasons for hiring men and women. As a rule, male employees are expected to supervise, analyze, make judgments, come up with ideas, and execute plans. Although many men begin at the bottom with low pay, they are trained and gradually promoted, with salary increases. Women, by contrast, are

hired primarily to assist men and are valued primarily for
their ability to organize, work cooperatively, and improve
office morale. They are given jobs that involve little training
and have few, if any, opportunities for advancement.

Thus, women, once hired, quickly discover that the fabled
Japanese policies of lifetime employment and slow but
steady promotion apply only to male workers. One woman
told me that, at her company, male employees had an
introductory training session at the company's summer
lodge even before they started working. Afterward, they
had another session that lasted several weeks, in addition
to on-the-job training from senior workers in their assigned
sections for the whole first year; they also had twice-a-week
English conversation lessons during work hours, paid for by
the company. In contrast, newly employed female workers
received a few days of seminars that covered office manners,
tea-serving, and how to take telephone messages.

Until recently, some companies had a written rule dictat-
ing a special retirement age for women, usually in the
mid-thirties. The practice of easing older women out the
company door, even without a written rule, was called
katatataki or "shoulder-tapping." A woman, for instance,
could be told by her employer (often with the insinuation
that she should marry before getting too old, etc.) that if
she were to think about quitting, her job could go to a
younger woman who has recently started as a temporary.
In larger industries in which employees are protected by
unions, shoulder-tapping might take a more subtle form, as
in the case of a woman whose story appeared weekly in the
women's column of *Asahi Shimbun* (4 June–10 September
1985).

A woman, age thirty-four, who had ten years of experience at one of the largest manufacturing firms was moved
to another much smaller department. In effect, she was
demoted. Although her work was simple—communicating
orders to various factories—and she was paid half of what

men in the same section received, this woman prided herself on maintaining accuracy and speed. When the company became computerized, she even took courses on her own initiative, mastering the new technology. For some time, she had been promised "men's work," such as making decisions on shipping merchandise, choosing methods of transport, and the like, which were all easy for her. Since she had been excited about the promise, her demotion felt like a betrayal. Some in this woman's situation have persevered and learned to live with such treatment, but many others resign, becoming weary of an environment unsympathetic or even hostile toward women.

Obvious discrimination against women is now against the law, but various forms of shoulder-tapping are still going on, such as employing part-time temporary workers and putting regular employees next to them in order to test the efficiency and drive of the regular workers. Automation can have a similar effect since it has made many jobs simpler, requiring little training or prior experience; old timers can now be easily replaced by women sent from a temporary agency. Shoulder-tapping happens because, in Japan, wages are based not so much on skill and performance as on the number of years spent at a company. It is a way to achieve a cheaper circulating labor force and is grossly unfair to the increasing number of women who take their work seriously.

If a woman continues to work despite an unsympathetic environment, she is more likely to experience discrimination in the area of promotion. A 1985 study by the Labor Bureau showed that, among the companies that hired new college graduates, half of them guaranteed women no promotion and no position change. Among those that did promote women (in fields like finance, insurance, real estate, and the service industries), one-third limited the promotions to the lowest level of management, *kakarichō* (section chief). In 1985, although 34 percent of all wage-earning workers in Japan were women, fewer than 1 percent of them were in management-level positions; there was no difference even in industries, such as banking and insurance, where women employees predominated. Japanese women have slowly been moving up.[6] Nevertheless the number of women in management is still dismally low; furthermore, most of them head sections in areas that are not vital to the primary business of the company—training and education, public relations, and research. Those who make it into management are mostly single and have worked for the company for many years.

Consider the case of my friend Hirose Yoshiko, a veteran editor in the publishing section of a large corporation. I remember her exhilaration, twenty-five years ago, when her career started taking off. At fifty, however, Yoshiko is still an "assistant to the editor-in-chief," a title created just for her. The men who began working at the magazine the same year as she and those who came after her have all been promoted. Now she suffers from a deep depression. "It's really tough to continue for another ten years to retirement, knowing that you're in a dead-end alley," she says. From her experiences, she knows that promotion comes only in the following order: capable man, incapable man, capable woman. As a result, the discrepancy between male and female wages persists. The average wage of women in 1990 was 57.1 cents for every dollar earned by men. (The discrepancy was smallest in 1975, when women earned 58.9 cents for each dollar men made, a considerable improvement from 45 cents in 1965.)

Professional women in various fields also face obstacles in their career development. In a survey of women doctors (about 10 percent of the total number of physicians in 1984), for example, nearly 80 percent of the respondents stated that they had experienced discriminatory treatment while receiving training, practicing medicine, or doing research.[7] In the field of education, the situation was similar, and, although male and female elementary and secondary teachers were paid the same wages, administrative positions were and still are dominated by men—only 2 percent of elementary school principals were female by 1987. At the college level, especially at top public universities, women instructors are severely underrepresented. At the University of Tokyo, where female student enrollment was about 10 percent, there were only two female full professors in 1984 (about 0.2 percent of the entire faculty).[8]

The slow progress for Japanese women at the workplace reflects not only employers' resistance to change but also an ambivalence among female college graduates. Although many express a desire for a career, they do not follow the necesary path or they give up after a few years on the job. Society, as embodied by a woman's mother, often encourages a woman to think about a future career while she is at school, but when a woman reaches her mid-twenties, the traditional attitude, that woman's happiness lies in a good marriage, prevails. The kind of education that women tend to receive is also a deterrent. Although the statistical figures make it appear that Japanese women are as well educated as men, Japan actually ranks low among industrial nations when one looks at the percentage of women receiving a four-year college education.[9] Furthermore, Japanese women, like those elsewhere, tend to study the humanities, education, and the social sciences—despite the fact that a science major would be more likely to lead to a high-paying job.[10]

Now that fewer women are leaving work to marry or to have children, many Japanese employers have somewhat improved their hiring and promotion practices. An acute labor shortage, which started during the 1980s, encouraged business and industry to consider young women with career ambitions and drive more seriously. More women are now working as much from a sense of independence, self-worth, and career commitment as out of economic necessity. Along with an increase in the number of professional women (in both traditional and new lines of work, such as sports and writing), there are more women working in fields, such as engineering and public safety, that had formerly been totally closed to them.[11] A definite increase in the number of women employees has been seen in growing businesses such as systems engineering, public relations, securities, and marketing. By the late 1980s, some Japanese career women even seem to have become afflicted with the malady of the nation's businessmen: the workaholic syndrome. An increasingly common sight on commuter trains—never seen ten years ago—is a businesswoman reading spread sheets and company reports.

Until recently, for Japanese women who desired serious jobs, one of the best opportunities was to learn English and work for foreign-owned companies (along with aiming at the management level in government work, for which stiff competition was open to women as well). Foreign companies offered good salaries, and, still unable to attract the best male workers (who were reluctant to work for non-Japanese firms), they turned to talented women.

Following the example of such foreign companies, some major Japanese firms, particularly department stores, airlines, and fashion and cosmetic companies, have recently become eager to tap the underused resources of women workers; they now recognize the invaluable perspectives and skills that women can bring to a company. When it comes to understanding consumers and clients, businesses have seen that women often surpass men. Therefore, department stores, for instance, cannot afford *not* to hire women as buyers, sales consultants, and in other key decision-making positions.

This awareness lay behind the decision made by Seibu Department Stores, one of the more progressive companies, to develop a rehiring system. Under this system, women employees with good records who leave to have children can come back and receive credit for their previous work (an important point under the current Japanese system in which the total years of employment count a great deal). This way, management can secure capable and experienced female employees as future candidates for managerial positions.

Other changes have also been favorable to career-minded women. With the growing realization that younger male workers are less inclined to follow in the footsteps of older generations of corporate employees and that they are less ambitious and harder to mold into a traditional pattern, more companies are not necessarily requiring long-term commitments from their employees as they have done in the past. Instead, they are now looking to a group of bright and ambitious women as well as men. Through more frequent visits abroad and through increasing business contacts with foreign firms, Japanese executives are learning to adjust their traditional views about employing women. For example, *Yomiuri Shimbun* now hires ten or more women reporters every year, although, in 1962 a woman like Fukai Tokiko, who had a degree from the prestigious University of Tokyo, was expected to do nothing more challenging than filing papers.[12]

These changes partly reflect the growing shortage of younger male workers as well as the passage of equal employment opportunity laws (of which more later). Particularly in industries such as insurance, where job performance can be clearly measured, women have been able to show their worth and are receiving promotions to managerial positions.

More and more career-minded women in Japan today carefully choose the field in which they want to work, and they are attracted to those firms where they can fulfill their potential. Like their American counterparts, these women, though still few in number, pursue career development by selling their skills and ambition; they may change employers as opportunities arise. Saitō Kiyomi, whose story appeared in a U.S. weekly magazine, *Parade* (9 June 1985) is a good example.

With a bachelor's degree in economics from Keio University, Saitō was employed by a newspaper. After she left this first job, she went to the United States; upon her return, she landed the job of secretary to the president of the Sony Corporation. Saitō believes that she was able to get this job because, being divorced, people thought she would not quit easily. Realizing that her job had no future (for, despite its international image, Sony is, after all, a Japanese firm), Saitō then went back to the United States and earned an M.B.A. from Harvard University. With this degree, she took a position at the Tokyo branch of the Bank of America as a management trainee; she left this company to work for Elizabeth Arden, and, then, for Morgan Stanley. Saitō's ultimate goal is to join a large Japanese company as its director—not an impossible aspiration, as demonstrated by the examples of Ishihara Ichiko of Takashimaya department store and of Baba Teiko of the Daiē supermarket chain, both directors of large corporations.

Increasing numbers of women currently in management believe in the possibility of changing the existing system and of developing new work habits and desirable management styles based on their own strengths. Some even believe that they can potentially demonstrate strengths in areas where women have been thought particularly weak, such as decision making and logical approaches to business. This belief has produced networking groups composed of women, such as the Association of Women Executives and the Group of Women Analysts. In the traditional climate of Japanese business, where quick decision making is deemphasized (where men need to go to bars and spend a great deal of time and energy trying to reach a consensus), women, who cannot be included in time-consuming off-work activities, may indeed come up with new ideas and do a better job in executing them in different ways than their male counterparts do.

Amid the favorable changes for women at the workplace, many issues still remain. After having interviewed women in managerial and executive positions in 1989, Takenobu Mieko, a reporter, came to the conclusion that a fundamental change in attitude is necessary. Besides a cultural prejudice against women managers, she believes, the traditional attitude of "men come first" has to be eliminated.[13] The common Japanese belief that good management requires not only ability and commitment but a harmonious family life, she says, also makes it difficult for a single career woman to pursue promotion into management.

Japanese career women on the whole are optimistic about their future opportunities, but there are some who advise caution. Promoting a few women to management and making them compete with men, says labor economist Shinotsuka Eiko, is a new corporate strategy. It is only those who are as ambitious as men and those who seem to be more capable than men, however, who are being recruited for management positions.[14]

When the United Nations "Decade of Women" ended in 1985 with a declaration urging countries to eliminate employment discrimination against women, the Japanese government ratified the declaration, and passed an Equal Employment Opportunity Law (EEOL), effective the following year. Throughout that year, there were heated exchanges between various women's groups and representatives of business and industrial management. I followed the argument in newspaper and magazine articles, and it went something like this:

Employers: We cannot promote women and give them more responsible jobs because they quit after a few years to get married.

Women: We admit some women do, but more of us want to continue working now. When we do stay on, we are discouraged by nasty remarks and subtle hints. And, because our jobs are often boring and unchallenging, it is not difficult to quit.

Employers: The fact remains that we cannot invest in someone who is not likely to be with us a long time. Our employees are not paid only for the specific jobs they perform. We expect a lifetime commitment.

Women: We are ready to make that commitment, but we should not be penalized, for example, for taking time off to have a child. If children are our future, is it not industry's responsibility to help make it easier to raise those children?

Employers: It does not seem right to pay the same salary to those who take time off and fall behind and those who do not.

Women: Considering the long hours Japanese men tend to work and the fact that most child rearing and housework is done by women, it is obviously not possible for us to work ten to fourteen hours a day.

Employers: But hard work is our most important national asset. Japan has almost no natural resources. We must rely on hard work and efficiency in order to survive in the world economy.

Attempts by Japanese women to improve working conditions had begun long before the EEOL, more than twenty years ago; both the equality of individuals and the right to work were guaranteed for all Japanese in the 1946 Constitution. During the 1960s, for instance, several legal battles were fought against company rules that discriminated against women. One woman, for example, took her employer, a manufacturing firm, to court because of the mandatory retirement age—thirty—it set for women.[15] Although the firm maintained that the presence of older, unmarried women "lowered morale and productivity," this woman won her case. In the 1970s, women challenged wage discrepancies, and many won their suits as well. Most women who litigated, in fact, won their cases. The process, however, is extremely time-consuming. A librarian's case, for example, filed in 1973, was not decided until 1986. Furthermore, courtroom confrontations come at the expense of company harmony. In the Japanese workplace, where smooth interpersonal relations are highly prized, filing suit, particularly for women, requires a good deal of courage.

Since passage of the EEOL, it is illegal to advertise jobs by sex and age, to have different hiring standards for men and women, and to limit on-the-job training to men. The law also states that discrimination against women in company retirement and dismissal policies is not allowed. Although a step in the right direction, this legislation was still merely a recommendation of equality, without legal provisions for enforcement, such as penalties for violation. Many companies, however, have shown an interest in complying. In October 1987, just over a year after the law went into effect, a study showed that nearly all industries surveyed had promised to eliminate some of their discriminatory hiring practices.

Instead of dividing work into male and female tasks, some companies, particularly large corporations in the insurance and securities industries, are now giving employees the choice of taking one of two paths: sōgō, or "comprehensive" (formerly "male"), and ippan, or "general" (formerly "female"). Not too surprisingly, just 20 percent of women have chosen the comprehensive path; nonetheless, it is a sizable number, considering that, in the past, almost 100 percent of women employees have automatically been put in clerical positions.

Although choosing the comprehensive path is difficult for a woman who has to balance career and family responsibilities, the EEOL benefits single women or women with cooperative spouses, giving them more opportunities. A single woman in her late twenties at a large securities firm, whose ultimate goal was to become a company executive, for example, opted to be on the comprehensive path. Having by then worked for a year as an "office lady," doing routine clerical work with the rest of the women, she took the written exams; although she did not pass the first time, she succeeded the second. Her new job involved hiring and training saleswomen for company branches throughout the country, and she now averages two to four hours of overtime a day.

In banks, brokerage firms, and the insurance industry, women like this are proving that they can compete with men. In response, Japanese industries are becoming more interested in hiring women as long-term employees; Tōshiba Electric, for instance, hired forty women (along with 200 men) in the comprehensive category as part of its new class of recruits of 1987. (Tōshiba also hired 150 female graduates with science degrees for its technical division.) These women, who were chosen from nearly 4,000 applicants, will now be able to compete with their male colleagues for promotion.

Despite such positive changes, however, overall employment patterns remain well entrenched. Males, who are automatically on the comprehensive track, do not have to take exams, but female candidates do. Company recruiters often try to discourage women, stressing the potential hardship of going comprehensive—the travel, transfers, overtime—and emphasizing that the course is not meant for those who want to have a family. Perhaps because they sense this lack of enthusiasm on the part of management, many women do not pursue the new opportunity; others chose the general course because it involves less pressure, is easier to quit, and sometimes, with the belief that women are best at clerical work. Furthermore, successful entry into the comprehensive course does not seem to guarantee the same bright future for a woman as for a man. According to a 1988 survey, in fact, 70 percent of 942 large corporations still envisioned women's highest promotion to be only to *kachō*, a section chief, which is one step above *kakarichō*.

In a 1991 poll, conducted by the Tokyo metropolitan government, some of the women surveyed (employees in the private sector) reported that promotions, as well as starting salaries, are still influenced by gender. Four years after the EEOL was put in practice, women employees, both in management and general staff, found no appreciable improvement.[16] Some considered the changes mere tokenism, while others thought that women on comprehensive were expected to function as a social "lubricant," to smooth the frictions between management and the clerical staff on the general course. It has also been reported that women in the comprehensive course sometimes have to deal with the envy and jealousy of female workers in the general course. Other perceived difficulties include having to compete with other women for the few managerial positions open to them, not being taken seriously by male colleagues, and feeling uncomfortable in the position of an "honorary male." Some women have lasted on the comprehensive track only a few years.

Some even argue that the EEOL is, in the end, detrimental to women. The loss of protective measures is sometimes a problem, particularly in unhealthy or hazardous environments. Under the EEOL, certain regulations applying only to women—limiting their work hours and restricting certain dangerous occupations—were eliminated; the prohibition of late night work was also lifted. On the one hand, these changes work to the advantage of some women: Female taxi drivers, for example, benefit because they can now work late at night, when profits are greater; when pressed by deadlines, a woman editor now can also work longer hours without worrying about stringent overtime regulations. Because protective measures for women (set up during the years immediately after the end of World War II) are not completely without value, the EEOL has met with opposition from various women's and professional groups, including the Japanese Association of Physicians.

Some people also have concerns that the EEOL will encourage the practice of shoulder-tapping; they fear that, because the new law pressures employers to pay women better wages, companies will want to get rid of older women after a few years and to hire cheaper entry-level women or temporary employees. The EEOL can benefit a company by subtly pressuring male workers into competing with highly ambitious and capable female workers on the comprehensive track. It may also result in polarizing women into either fiercely ambitious career women, who are willing to sacrifice marriage and family life to keep up with men, or the traditional "office lady" employees.

Others go so far as to hold the cynical view that lifting protective measures under the EEOL was intended to encourage women with family responsibilities to drop out of the work force. Kusunose Mikiko, mentioned in Chapter 4, works at a demanding job in advertising and raises her two children with the help of a day-care service and hiring a neighbor. Her husband told her that her working did not seem worth the trouble. Another woman, with a two-year-old daughter and a husband who considers her work nothing more than a hobby, negotiated with management to work one hour less, from 9:00 to 4:20, so that she can make it to the day-care center. This was possible because she works at a small company; this means however, that her salary is below average.

It is simply impossible for Japanese women who are also homemakers to put in the same hours as men (who are in the habit of working an average of 580 hours a year more than Swedish men, for example, and who consider housework and child rearing a woman's job). Particularly, mothers of small children, who nowadays have less chance of enlisting relatives to help them and have a longer commute time to work, are finding it extremely difficult to keep full-time jobs.

According to 1991 statistics, close to 7 million Japanese households, like that of Mikiko, had both parents employed, or slightly more than one-third of the total number of two-parent households with children.[17] The number of such households has been increasing every year. Unfortunately, finding adequate child-care continues to be a big hurdle.

Japanese mothers have access to child care through government-authorized day-care centers, but most centers require parents to pick up their child between 4:00 and 6:00 pm; sometimes mothers initially have to spend a part of the day at the center until their child becomes used to the new environment. In order to protect young children's welfare, the law prohibits these centers from keeping a child for more than eight hours; under pressure by women's groups, some centers are now open longer hours.[18] The scarcity of these centers, however, often necessitates that mothers apply in advance (sometimes as soon as they become pregnant). Centers that take babies less than a year old are extremely limited, and, while a single parent is given priority and can place a child without having a job, there is a time limit for her to find work. The lifestyles of women in Japan, as elsewhere, are changing, but the idea behind child care remains unchanged. The popular notion is still that mothers should work part time and only after their years of intensive child rearing are over. Compared with the situation in the United States, Japanese mothers have few alternatives since such arrangements as *au pairs* or neighborhood babysitting rarely exist.

Takenobu Mieko has concluded that having a child is rapidly becoming a luxury for working women in Japan. She interviewed women working at banks and in the securities and communication industries.[19] Motivated to identify the important factors that enable mothers to continue working, she found that many women have foregone motherhood in order to keep thier jobs. The recent low birthrate (1.66 children per woman in 1988, 1.54 in 1990), in Takenobu's opinion, is related to the difficulties and discouragement that working mothers are experiencing. Facing a labor shortage because of an aging population and a low birthrate, some businesses have encouraged women to leave home and enter the labor force. Still, many working mothers feel that the innovative programs offered by certain businesses either amount to token offerings or are available to only a select few.

In 1991, the government, seeking ways to increase the birthrate, passed the Child Care Leave Law. It guarantees working mothers (or fathers) the right to take up to one year off to take care of a newborn and also to consider shorter work days when such a leave is not taken. Like the EEOL, this law does not have any mechanisms for enforcement and is applicable only for full-time workers. As anticipated, the number of mothers who have taken advantage of this law is small. According to a Labor Ministry survey, slightly more than half the women workers would not take this long-term leave because of the discouraging atmosphere in the workplace; others are reluctant to put an extra burden on coworkers.[20]

Many Japanese mothers try to work full time, only to find that their dual role as housewife and employee is too exhausting. Some of these women conclude that work equality with men is not worth attaining. Others believe that the government wishes to encourage women with children to work part time rather than full time. What is needed, most working mothers agree, is a change in the working pattern of Japanese men, so that men can be motivated to take more responsibility at home. The rigid gender-role division has been on the agenda of many women's groups for some time

now as crucially important. It is necessary for the improvement of women's status at the workplace.

Despite obvious disadvantages in terms of salary and
benefits,[21] many women, particularly those with families,
prefer part-time arrangements not only because it is easier
to find such positions in an easy–commute location but also
because working hours are shorter and more flexible. With
no hope of their husbands and children helping with household chores, these women see full-time employment as unrealistic.

A housewife in her early forties who wrote in the reader's
column of *Kōbe Shimbun* in early 1987 reveals much about
the situation of part-timers. "I should get a job, I keep saying
to myself," the woman stated. She was physically fit and
therefore should be able to work for at least another fifteen
years. She hesitated when it came to taking the first step,
however; if she went to work, she could not perform chores
important to her, such as putting out the futons on nice days
to air for a few hours, and she would have to manage her
time much more rigorously. But she was still convinced that
some change was needed in her life: "My thoughts go round
and round and I find it difficult to make up my mind, but
unless I get out of the house now, I'll be too old soon." This
woman was expressing sentiments shared by a growing
number of Japanese housewives in recent years. She looked
around her and saw working wives everywhere. In 1985, for
the first time in the history of modern Japan, the number of
married women who worked outside the home surpassed
the number who did not; more than half of those who did
not have a job wanted to find one.

The women's magazine *Fujin Kōron* (*Women's Forum*) ran
several profiles of part-timers at the end of the 1980s. At
thirty-six, Atsuko decided to work when most of the other
members of her tennis group, neighborhood wives, began
working. Atsuko felt left out; her two children were busy
with after-school activities, and her husband was en-

grossed with his work. Earning her own income was an attractive idea. Atsuko got a job at a local department store, working twenty days a month for 70,000 yen ($560) after tax. Of that she spent 10,000 yen ($80) on clothes, 20,000 ($160) on socializing, and 30,000 ($240) on special household expenses. The remaining 10,000 ($80) went into savings.

Mayo, twenty-six, the mother of a small child, went to work at a food-processing company. Her husband's salary barely covered their basic expenses, and she also wanted to save money to afford a second child. Along with 120 other part-time women, Mayo worked five days a week from 9:00 to 4:00, earning 500 yen ($4) an hour. Out of the 60,000 yen ($480) she took home, she spent 13,000 yen ($104) on day care, 20,000 yen ($160) on herself and the household budget, and saved the rest.

Kazue had less obvious motivation to go to work. One winter morning, after doing the dishes and vacuuming, she fell asleep while reading the newspaper. Driven by a pang of guilt, Kazue decided to get a job at a new dry-cleaning shop in the neighborhood, earning 550 yen ($4.40) an hour. She intends to continue working until her parents or her husband's parents need more care.

Japanese wives now have good reason to work outside the home. There is a new and favorable image of working women in the media, the lure of extra pocket money, and more free time as well. According to one poll, women gave the following reasons for working: enrichment of personal life (41 percent), supplement of household income (36 percent), expression of individuality (15 percent), and simply getting out of the house (5 percent). One common aspect of the last reason is a desire to escape the demands of in-laws and to avoid unnecessary conflicts.

Most of the women who work have to combine family responsibilities with the demands of work, and therefore opt to work as part-timers, or *pāto*, as the Japanese say. The number of these women has increased fivefold since 1960, and, of about 3 million women part-timers, more than 80 percent are housewives. Although they are called part-timers, however, many womem work only slightly fewer hours than full-time workers. According to a 1986 study done by the Tokyo metropolitan government, more than half of the women part-timers worked six and sometimes even seven days a week; about one-third worked at least seven hours a day. Working in both manufacturing and service industries, more than two-thirds of the part-timers were employed in small-scale businesses where employees numbered fewer than 100.

Female part-timers are a source of cheap labor. Even though they work almost as many hours as full-timers, they make seventy-six cents for every dollar that full-timers make (the wage gap increased in 1990 to seventy-one cents to a dollar). If bonuses for full-timers (the equivalent of up to several months of salary commonly given to employees twice a year, depending on a company's profit) are included, the difference becomes greater. In economic hard times, part-timers can easily be cut back.

The number of women who work part time started to increase rather sharply during the economic slowdown of the early 1970s. With soaring inflation and little increase in husbands' salaries, extra income was necessary to maintain the standard of living, which had gone up during the previous decade. It was also around this time that the work once done by men was being simplified by automation, leaving many jobs open to women part-timers. Shinotsuka Eiko, a labor economist, however, has maintained that employing large numbers of part-timers was a corporate strategy conceived in the early 1970s.[22] Part-timers who could be easily hired and fired introduced a flexibility that the Japanese system of employment had not had before.

The number of women part-timers steadily increased during the subsequent years. In 1981, one out of every four women workers (one of twenty men) was a part-timer, but, in 1990, nearly one-third of the 18 million female employees were part-timers. According to Shinotsuka, one-third of these part-timers have no social security or health insurance benefits, and sometimes even no written contracts. About half have no paid vacation or pay raises.

The more commonly given reasons for choosing a part-time job still include flexibility of work hours and an easier commute. Nonetheless, substantial numbers of women have sought full-time positions but been unable to find them.[23] Business and industry clearly take advantage of women who, though they want to work full time, cannot do so for various reasons. Over the years, however, part-timers have become more vocal in expressing their needs, and, in 1981, a part-timers union was formed in Kyoto. Some labor unions have also begun including the needs of part-timers in their demands to management.

In 1993, in the middle of the post-bubble recession, however, part-timers are finding Shinotsuka's assessment to be accurate. A woman, age fifty-one, who had worked for an insurance company for eleven years, for instance, was suddenly told she had no job. The Tokyo Union of Community Workers, a part-timers union, received about 2,500 similar complaints that year.[24] The woman complained that employers have now "lost their traditional morality," for in the past they at least guaranteed work in return for workers' devotion. Many part-timers today share her sentiment.

Temporary employment, even more flexible than part-time work, has become more popular in Japan in recent years, resulting in a proliferation of employment agencies. Manpower Japan, the oldest temporary employment agency and a branch of a U.S. company, for example, had, in 1986, 10,000 names on its register; 98 percent of the registrants were women looking for jobs both in clerical and skilled work. Temporary Center, the largest agency with a file of

28,000 names, provides short-term training in word process-
ing and other office and interpersonal skills. Although temporary workers also do not receive bonuses or benefits, their
hourly pay scale is slightly better than that of regular full-
time employees and up to three and a half times higher than
that of nonskilled part-timers. Some who have highly developed skills, such as simultaneous translation, are paid
very well. As business and industry become ever more
computerized and specialized, temporary workers are often
hired to save the cost of training and retraining full-time
employees.[25]

As the number of people who obtain work through temporary employment agencies has increased (about 430,000
nationwide in 1991), the problems experienced by those
workers have become more prominent. When a hotline
was set up in Tokyo for two days in 1991, nearly 200 callers
used the opportunity to report such problems as sudden
dismissals and working conditions different from those in
the contract. It is reported that sometimes agencies charge
a commission that is as much as 60 percent of a worker's
pay.[26] The 1986 Manpower Dispatching Business Law evidently needs to be changed, as it does not at this point
enforce punishment for not following contracts.

For the bright and ambitious woman, an attractive alternative to making it in the corporative structure is self-
employment. It promises a certain satisfaction for women
who have been frustrated by an inflexible system and unsympathetic working environments. As a spirit of financial
independence has risen among Japanese women in general,
including housewives, some women have been encouraged
to venture into small businesses.

A few decades ago, woman-owned businesses were
limited largely to the "water trade"—bars and nightclubs.
More recently, a much broader range of activity has opened,
including small retail clothing or accessory stores, coffee
shops, and restaurants. Businesses can sometimes start with

as little as 1 million yen ($8,000) in capital. One woman who lives in a high-rise condominium, for instance, sells accessories and dolls on her veranda. Her merchandise is made by nine other women, all housewives, and she collects 20 percent of total sales. Although customers have to go up to the eighth floor and through the living room to the "store," she has a steady word-of-mouth clientele. Examples of women who have taken the plunge into enterprise abound, and, in the process, some have demonstrated both business savvy and innovation.

The success story of Okumura Reiko, a former flight attendant, was widely reported several years ago as an example of growing female entrepreneurship. Having worked for four years for Japan Air Lines, where women had a choice of two jobs (flight attendant or office clerk), Reiko quit to start a business with six other women—a shopping service for foreigners visiting Japan. After divorcing her husband, who had been skeptical and unsupportive throughout the early years of her business venture, Okumura put all her energy into her new business. She called it *Aru* (R), "R" standing for "revolution." Within a few years, and with new additional capital from her parents, Okumura developed the R Company first into an interpreting service and then into a temporary employment agency. She now has more than thirty employees and more than 650 registered temporary workers.

Another woman, Nishimura Namiko, benefited from the increasing need felt by companies in recent years to train women employees. She established a consulting firm that advises businesses on training and developing women employees. Ten years ago, according to Nishimura, on-the-job training for women was limited to teaching proper manners. But now, more firms want to train women as they do men, even to become potential managers. Lacking experience in dealing with women managers, they use Nishimura's services.

Some women are getting a head start in business while still in college; as early as 1984, there were a few dozen small business ventures begun and run by college women. In Osaka, "Temporary Express," the brainchild of Tanabe Hiroko, age twenty-two, delivered small packages within three to four hours. Tanabe, who employed young women as drivers of the company's "supermini" cars, was expanding the business to Tokyo. Tago Midori and two friends were students at Waseda University when they began a highly successful business conducting seminars on high-tech information and communications systems. In 1983, their company, Cosmopia, Inc., had sales of 20 million yen ($160,000) and counted among its clients top business executives from some of the largest corporations in Japan.

Other women own businesses even in traditionally male domains such as construction. Kume Mariko's construction company, which she inherited when her husband died suddenly, had sixteen employees. It was her sense of duty toward her late husband and the employees that made her decide to keep the business, against the advice of relatives and friends. The company has since expanded during a subsequent major construction boom. Companies headed by women presidents are increasing (reaching about 42,000 altogether in 1993), but most of them, like Kume's, are small- to medium-sized companies in which women have taken over a family business or succeeded their husbands.[27]

More commonly, women go into businesses that use their expertise as homemakers—cooking, cleaning, and other work around the house. Hanaichi, a box lunch business, for instance, was organized by three housewives in 1983. After they were written up in a local newspaper, business increased, and Hanaichi expanded its service to elderly people in senior day centers. Planning special events, such as women's festivals, and publishing *minikomi*, or small community papers, are other types of business ventures popular among women now. *Waifu*, a women's quarterly magazine, is one of the earliest and most successful efforts by housewives in publishing. Another group, *Bukkupawā* (Book Power), is a firm that promotes the sale of books. It was organized in 1982 by a group of ten housewives, led by a woman experienced in the book-selling business; by 1987, it had contracts with three major commercial publishers. Characteristically, these businesses start with group activities in areas that interest women, such as environmental protection and safer food, for example. As they run their businesses, the women expand their networks with other women and enhance their social and community awareness.

Many other women are involved in more traditional types of self-employment, such as giving lessons in English music, or other areas of arts and crafts. Turning hobbies into profitable businesses, or *hobijinesu* (a word coined from "hobby" and "business"), will continue to be popular among women in Japan, particularly among housewives.

This discussion of working women has not included blue-collar workers, those who work in farming and fishing, and women in small family-run stores. Women factory workers have been the backbone of Japan's industrial development since the end of the nineteenth century. Working long hours under extremely poor conditions, many paid a high price, especially in terms of ill health, and they learned early to join their male counterparts in union activity. These women have continued to contribute to the nation's industrial development, helping to build today's high-tech industries by assembling computers, televisions, cameras, and watches.

There are also many women who work in mom-and-pop shops and in small family-run restaurants. Faced with competition from the big all-purpose supermarkets and discount stores, family businesses still abound in Japanese cities—nearly 2 million of them. In 1987, when I lived in an Osaka suburb, I saw many small retail stores—a bakery, a bicycle shop, a book store, a small appliances store, and a liquor store, as well as a few restaurants—all within a few blocks from the apartment where we lived. Many of these were run by a husband-and-wife team. Although women in these family businesses let their husbands assume leadership in the business, I saw wives work as hard as their husbands, if not harder, and sometimes they seemed to have more business sense.

Forty years ago, more than 60 percent of Japanese working women toiled in the family business, which usually was farming. As of the late 1970s, the number of women in farming only made up less than 1 percent of the total female work force.[28] However, Japanese farming has come to depend a great deal on these women, since industrialization has took men away to cities and factories. Such women are now often left alone with their children and older family members to run farms in remote regions. Their husbands are gone to earn cash wages in some other work, so women must take on the responsibility of managing the farms as well as actually taking part in some of the labor. As a result, young farming women often are more independent than were those of older generations.

7

Women's Independence and Old Age

A few years ago, I came across a poem that revealed the predicament of some Japanese elderly people today. In this poem, entitled "Obāsan" ("Grandma"), a fifth-grade child from a small village in northern Japan tells how his grandmother has her turnips and radishes cooked for dinner in the traditional way while the rest of the family eats Western dishes. Although this grandmother lives with the family of her son, she feels alone. She also feels useless. Her mother and mother-in-law taught her how to cook, but now her *yome* (daughter-in-law) is not interested in learning from her.

I am reminded of my grandfather, who was happy during the postwar years participating in the daily task of food preparation. His job was to make fish balls, a necessary task that no one else wanted, since it required a laborious process of cleaning small bony fish and grinding the meat with a mortar and pestle. In his later years, my grandfather lost this job when we started buying ready-made fish balls. He went to live with the family of his eldest son, even though he knew that he did not get along with his daughter-in-law. The quick deterioration of his health and his peculiar behavior toward the end indicate that psychological factors may have influenced his death. His wife, who had more ways to help her three daughters keep house, was active and cheerful longer than he, but, as her health declined, she too went to live with the family of her eldest son, despite the drawbacks.

My paternal grandmother decided differently. Unlike my maternal grandparents, who followed the common practice of living with the family of the eldest son, she, a long-time widow with comfortable income of her own, chose to live with her daughter's family. Until she died at ninety-nine, she led a life of good health and a considerable sense of autonomy. She stays in my memory as a person who read the newspaper every morning and gave handsome gifts of money whenever I visited her.

My mother's situation has been different yet. Now almost eighty years old, she has experienced a great deal of change in her psychological and economic life over four decades. Thirty-seven years ago when she suddenly found herself a widow with two teen-age children, she summoned enough courage to find a bookkeeping job, without any previous training or experience; after working until retirement, she started to enjoy life with a degree of affluence unimagined by her or even by her daughter, who was used to the American standard of living. She continues to live with her only son, who for various reasons has remained single. She went through many years of worry over the matter of her son's not marrying, until it became clear to her and to everyone else concerned that he chose not to have a wife; my mother was thus saved from the challenge of living with a daughter-in-law. Considerably freer than her friends who had husbands, she has enjoyed various hobbies, including traveling and gourmet dining, to her heart's content until the past few years, when age began to limit her activities. In exchange for her freedom, however, she gained the uncertainty as to who would care for her when she becomes bed-ridden. My brother, like most Japanese men, is not likely to do the job.

As in my mother's case, those elderly women in Japan today who are blessed with relatively good health and financial independence actively seek each other's company (most of the time without their spouses), something their elders had seldom done. Judging from the number of advertisements for recreational activities aimed at this age group, including traveling abroad, one can see that they have ample opportunities to have a good time.

But only as long as they are physically and mentally independent. One of my mother's best friends looked after her husband who suffered from a complicated medical condition followed by behavior problems caused by dementia. This meant the loss of all free time and energy to enjoy herself. Since her only child's family lives in another part of the country, she had to struggle by herself until her son decided to come to stay with his parents, returning to see his own family only occasionally. Another family friend, a long-time widow who was determined to live with her only son and his wife, built a semi-detached house where two households could live very closely but independently. Her son chose to marry a woman who would not agree to this living arrangement. Since her son's second marriage and another attempt with a similar ending, the woman lives alone, in declining health; she copes by using hired help. The last time I talked to my mother, she intimated that she is counting on her niece, a single woman in her late forties who had looked after her sickly mother until her death fifteen years earlier, for final assistance.[1]

The Japanese population is aging at a rapid rate. Those who are over 65 exceeded 7 percent of the population in 1970 and currently represent 11.6 percent. This rate of increase is almost twice as fast as that in the United Kingdom, which has the world's second highest rate of aging. In Japan today, there is a man or woman (sometimes both) aged sixty-five or older in nearly a quarter of all households.

Confucian doctrine regarding filial piety has taught the Japanese over many years that children should put their parents' welfare before their own. Although the nuclear family is a relatively recent phenomenon in Japan (in the 1960s, roughly a third of all households contained three generations), the increasing life expectancy (currently the longest in the world) and the decreasing number of births in recent years (dropped to 1.4 per woman in 1993) have made traditional three-generational living difficult. The Japanese elderly today are confronted with the need to alter their expectations about living arrangements.

And yet, a 1990 study by the Prime Minister's Office showed that nearly 60 percent of elderly Japanese women (compared to 3.5 percent in the United States) believed that living under the same roof with their child's family is the best way to spend their later life. If they do not live with them, they tend to stay away from their children. According to the above study, only slightly more than one-third of elderly Japanese women (compared to two-thirds of American elderly women) saw their children more than once a week. The sentiment that children who do not live with their parents are not to be relied upon is still strong. The same study also showed that more than twice as many Americans as Japanese depended upon friends and acquaintances for help in illness in old age.

Traditionally, it was the eldest son who was responsible for the welfare of elderly parents, an obligation that came to him together with the right to inherit the household. The Japanese expectation that the eldest son—but in practical terms—his wife—would look after his aged parents persisted even after World War II, when the law changed, making inheritance equitable among all children. Although their number has been decreasing, many elderly Japanese still feel that they should live with their eldest sons' families when they can no longer take care of themselves; they expect their financial, social, and emotional security to be provided there. Roughly one-third of elderly Japanese do live with their sons' families (compared to 8.6 percent living with their daughters'), and most expect their *yome* (daughter-in-law) to look after them when they become ill and unable to take care of themselves. This is the background for the following incident, which was reported in various Japanese newspapers; popular responses varied.

In February 1984, the Japanese press carried the story of a ninety-year-old man from Yokohama who had strangled his bed-ridden wife. The couple had lived alone, and the husband was distraught, having looked after his sick wife for an extended period of time. Because of his advanced age and the circumstances of the crime, the old man was released without charge but not until his *yome* offered to look after him. In response to the court's decision, a housewife, age twenty-six, wrote to the newspaper as follows: "Why is it always the *yome* who is expected to look after aged parents?" She resented the implication given in the article that the incident in Yokohama could have been avoided if the elderly couple had lived with their son and his wife, with the *yome* taking care of her sick mother-in-law.[2]

Nevertheless, some questioning is occurring in Japan, as can be seen in the following quotes from articles in a 1987 women's magazine (*Fujin Kōron*). In a readers' contribution column entitled "Our Honest Wishes," women in their early sixties revealed their hopes and plans for their old age. One wrote:

If I tell my honest feelings, I don't want my two sons [and their wives—author's note] to look after me in my old age. When each became engaged, I was told later, the wife–to–be made it a condition that I and my husband wouldn't live with them. I was hurt, naturally, but kept a hope that they might change their minds if they have children. . . . . We have enough savings and income from our pension so that we could opt to go to a private nursing home, but my hope now is my daughter. She is still a college student, but I hope she'll marry a salaried businessman, and I want them to live in the large house we own. I am sure we can get along well. I don't want her to marry someone who is an only son; I want to save her from having to deal with her in-laws. I realize my contradiction, but. . . .

A second woman stated: "When my husband dies, I plan to return to my own hometown in Hiroshima, where my brother has a farming machinery business; I get along well with my nephew and his wife there." This writer, age sixty-three, had two sons and a daughter, each of whom sent money to help her and her husband, who was very ill. She, however, had learned to accept that they were busy with their own lives, and, judging from their infrequent visits and general lack of interest in their parents, she had decided that she could not depend on them.[3]

A third woman was also not counting on her eldest son. Although she agreed with the common sentiment that aged parents should live with the family of the eldest son, particularly "if he has a secure job at a large and reputable firm," she knew she did not get along with her eldest son's wife. Her second son was not stable financially. Unlike the other two writers, this woman felt strongly that the government should look after her. Her husband had narrowly escaped death as a young air force combat officer, and, after he retired, he worked in building maintenance because all of his retirement money had gone to pay off their mortgage. "We are the generation who served the country more than anybody else," she stated; she felt that she and her husband were entitled to a government-run home for the aged.

Although the idea of the three-generational family promotes an impression of harmony, these writers and various studies indicate that old people who live with their families are not necessarily more likely to be happy than those who do not. Suicide among the elderly in three-generational households, for instance, is just as frequent as among those who live by themselves.[4]

In his book, *Moete-tsukitashi* (*Want to Keep Yearning till the End*, 1984), reporter and author Saitō Shigeo wrote about an old woman who took her life while living with the family of her eldest son. The mountain village in northern Japan where this woman lived is known for its high incidence of suicide among the elderly; having lost a considerable number of residents to large cities, the villages in the area are ahead of the national trend of aging, with the population over age sixty-five having reached nearly 27 percent. The old woman, Fusa, hanged herself in the next-door neighbor's house, which had been vacant since they left the village several years earlier. Her husband, born in extreme poverty, had worked in various construction jobs all his life and was still working, at age seventy-nine, with his daughter-in-law on a farm. Her son had a steady job at a local construction company. Fusa had three grandchildren, and the house, thanks to income from the son's work, was full of modern conveniences. Fusa's note, addressed to her daughter-in-law, simply stated an apology and best wishes for the young couple. There was no clue as to the cause of her suicide, other than that, not being very strong, she may have felt guilty among the other family members who worked hard.

No one can say if having a friend might have helped. A 1990 comparative study, by the Prime Minister's Office, of the social life of the elderly shows that elderly Japanese women are much less active than their American counterparts in religious and other social group activities. Elderly Japanese women (and men) reported that they had no friends at a rate five times higher than that of their American counterparts. Though increasing in recent years, the involvement of elderly Japanese women in various kinds of volunteering, one route to friendships, remains small (only slightly more than one-quarter of the population, about half the rate in the United States).

In 1982, 600 participants, including working women, housewives, institutional care providers, and volunteers, gathered in Tokyo for a symposium called "Women's Independence and Old Age."[5] This was the first time that Japanese women had gotten together in such a format to share their experiences.

Many problems of the kinds one might expect were shared. Having finished raising her children, one woman said, she was finally able to go back to work, only to find that taking care of a sick in-law would require more of her time than child care had. A single woman who had been looking after her ninety-year-old mother for a long time told of the difficulty of being both the breadwinner and the only caregiver. A housewife who looked after her own parents as well as her husband's described her life as "hell," with its constant lack of sleep, piles of laundry, tension, and total exhaustion. Yet another woman said that, after eleven years of silent struggle in taking care of her elderly parents, she reached the conclusion that she would like to be a man in her next life.

Among those who see it as their responsibility to take care of aged parents at home are women who are prepared to quit their jobs to do so. In a 1988 study (by the Employment Research Agency), more than 40 percent of working women had changed jobs or shortened their working hours in order to look after their aged parents or husbands; more than half of those surveyed stated that, if they were needed to look after their family members, they would not be able to continue their employment. A woman who worked at a telephone company stated that many of her colleagues assumed that they were responsible for providing care for their parents—on whom some of them had depended for child care earlier; not a few women in their mid-fifties had actually already left work to do so.[6] In 1992, the government introduced and passed legislation to enable employees to take time off (up to six months without pay) not only to care for children but for sick or frail parents as well.[7]

To make matters more complicated, Japan is expected to continue to be short of laborers (in 1989, the Ministry of Labor predicted a shortage of at least 4 million by the year 2005). This would result in fewer wives staying at home to care for their in-laws. The Japanese government has traditionally promoted the desirability of home care over institutionalized care and emphasized the notion that one of the inherent functions of the family is to take care of its members. The government now realizes that such an approach is not going to meet the need. It is projected that, by year 2000, people over seventy will reach 10 percent of the entire population (those over sixty-five will reach 20 percent by 2011) and that those who need care will by then be more than 1 million (currently 600,000). Hence, in 1988, the government announced a ten-year *gōrudo puran*, or "gold plan," as it is called. Having started in 1990, the plan emphasizes home-based care programs, such as "home-helper" services, hot lunch delivery, respite care, and day centers for the aged.

In September 1993 and again in March 1994, *Asahi Shimbun* serialized special articles reporting on some examples of newly developed home-based care programs for the elderly. The city of Yokohama now contracts home-helper services from an organization that employs 3,000 part-time *herupā* ("helpers"). As *Asahi Shimbun* explained, a client of this service, one Mrs. Tsugihara, who was partially paralyzed due to a stroke, could stay at home, despite her daughter's working full time. A college student helper takes Mrs. Tsugihara out every morning for an hour and a half, then, while Mrs. Tsugihara rests, the student vacuums and does other housework until the daughter returns home at 6:00. Mrs. Tsugihara could have these services—about thirty hours a week, costing about 100,000 yen ($900) a month—covered by her pension. Her daughter, who had just returned to full-time work after intensive child-rearing years, did not have to quit her job.

A Dr. Aoki started a "Visiting Nurse Station" to extend the services of his clinic-hospital, which had nineteen beds in 1993. Because of this, one patient has been able to return home after having stayed at the hospital for eight years because of severe arthritis. "The Station" visits her twice a week and provides basic nursing, monitoring, and bathing. The Aoki Clinic, in addition to "Station" and hospital care, offers day services, such as sending a microbus to bring patients to receive meal service, medical check-ups, and rehabilitation and recreational programs). The cost of sending for the "Nurse Station" is 250 yen ($2.20) a visit, and those over age seventy (or sixty-five, if bed-ridden) can use health insurance for the aged to cover the service.

A few cities in Japan have also started round-the-clock helper services and can send a pair of helpers every three hours throughout the night so that not-so-healthy caregivers can at least sleep through the night. Designed primarily to assist elderly people who have severe dementia with toileting, each visit takes less than ten minutes, and the cost of care is considerably less than institutionalization.

The suburban city of Musashino, near Tokyo, where the proportion of the population over age sixty is quite high, this home-based care has been available since 1981. There, old people can receive meal service, visiting nurses, and sometimes round-the-clock help; for those who lack the funds to pay for such services, the city offers interest-free loans, with the patient's house as collateral, an ingenious idea for Japanese cities, in which the value of houses is very high. When a friend from Musashino told me that she had no worry for her old age, she was referring to this system. Even if she needed services for a rather extended period of time, she said, the value of her house (which she owns outright) would cover the cost nicely.

The National Health Insurance Plan, which was over-hauled in 1958, covers virtually all Japanese. Under this system, the insured bears 30 percent of costs when the amount is over 54,000 yen ($550 at the 1993 exchange rate) a month, and the rest is covered by the insurance. Insured retirees and their dependents receive 80 percent coverage on medical care. In 1973, new legislation was introduced to provide free medical services—doctor visit, medicine, hospitalization—for people over seventy (and for the bed-ridden, those over sixty-five). The high cost of such care, however, led to modifications in 1982 (the Health Care for the Aged law), whereby small co-payments are required. Under this law, local governments have to issue a "health pocketbook" to the elderly. By requiring that this booklet be presented by the patient in order to receive care, over-laps or conflicts in services can be eliminated, cutting down medical costs.

Ninety percent of the elderly in Japan who are over sixty-five and live home include those (approximately two-thirds) with poor health and other problems such as dementia. Two-thirds of those who need round-the-clock care are looked after by women, mainly daughters-in-law; the rest are in hospitals and nursing homes. "Oi no michi, onna no michi" ("The Way of Old Age, The Way of Women"), a series that appeared in *Yomiuri Shimbun* during 1984, portrayed various situations in which old people with dementia were looked after at home, mostly by daughters-in-law. One story was as follows.

Yukie and her husband finally decided to take Yone in after Yone exhibited various symptoms of dementia, rang-ing from getting lost in the neighborhood to causing a fire in her room. A mother who had raised two sons single-hand-edly and lost one when the war was almost at an end, Yukie felt there was no option but to live with and take care of Yone, although she was not an easy *shūtome* (mother-in-law) to serve. Yukie persevered, however, for nearly thirty years.

When Yukie's own health began rapidly failing and she became distressed to the point of thinking of taking both her own life and Yone's, she realized that she had no choice but to place Yone in an institution. Even then, she stated that she was reluctant and extremely sad.

Most Japanese of Yukie's generation are familiar with the story of *Ubasute*, a legend frequently found in mountain regions in Japan, in which a son takes his aged mother to the mountain on the day of the first snowfall to leave her there to wait for her death. It was a practice not uncommon in the old days. *Narayama bushi kō* (*The Song of Narayama*), a novel by Fukazawa Schishiro that was subsequently made into a film, is based on this practice. Yukie and her husband could not help associating their actions with the legend. Now that I am approaching my own old age, Yukie told a reporter, I keep thinking of how to avoid causing difficulties for my only son.

As the number of old people has increased, providing the necessary care for them, as Yukie did, is becoming more difficult. Many young women are reluctant to marry an oldest son, knowing that the traditional practice of caring for aged parents at home has been largely on the shoulders of daughters-in-law. Although people now realize that this idea of family responsibility is unrealistic, a *yome*'s relationship to her in-laws remains a highly sensitive matter in Japan.

Nursing homes for elderly people who need round-the-clock care are relatively new in Japan, with a history of less than three decades. Even in 1988, the total number of such facilities was about 2,500 in the entire country.[8] Institutionalization was necessary for the residents of nursing homes because no other caregivers were available. Understandably, more than two-thirds of the residents are women.

The overall lack of adequate public services has recently allowed business to develop a so-called "silver" industry (referring to gray, or the elderly), consisting of privately run

nursing and retirement homes and various types of insurance. All of these are quite costly, enabling only a small
minority to benefit.[9]

When I was a child, these institutions were called *yōrōin*
and had a distinctly negative connotation, similar to that of
an orphanage. As residents of such institutions became less
likely to be pitied, and as the name was changed to *rōjin
hōmu*, or home for the aged, the image has improved. Even
so, people's perceptions (and the reality) of these institutions
are far from favorable. My mother, for example, used to say
casually that, since she did not want to tax her children in
her old age, she planned to go to *rōjin hōmu*. When she
reached mid-seventy, however, she seemed to change her
mind and stopped mentioning the idea entirely. A friend's
mother-in-law, who had a habit of bringing up *rōjin hōmu* as
a solution to the slightest conflicts at home, did the same
when her son once uttered his agreement.

Although community involvement and budgetary support of various programs for the elderly are slowly improv-
ing, the problem of a graying society at this point is still
very much a women's problem. There is an old expression
in Japan: Women live old age three times—first taking care
of their parents-in-law, then their husbands, and finally,
themselves. While women in their late fifties continue to
feel that it is their obligation to look after their in-laws,
many women cannot do so, given their commitment to
work. In the face of rising numbers of elderly people, the
Japanese are groping for some solution that will put less of
the burden on women.

8

Wūman Ribu and the Women's Movement in Japan

On October 21, 1970, the International Day Against Wars, careful observers might have noticed that among the demonstrators on the streets of Ginza, Tokyo, was a group of women carrying placards that were a bit different from the others. They read, for example, "What's feminine?" or "Mom, does marriage really make me happy?" The placards were signs of change, announcing the beginning of the women's movement in Japan.

Three weeks later, on November 14, a women's gathering held in Tokyo attracted some media attention. Called "A Forum for Liberation and Indictment of Sexism," the gathering was organized by several women's groups, including *Gurūpu: Tatakau Onna* (Group: Women Who Fight) and *Josei Kaihō Junbikai* (Committee Preparing for Women's Liberation), both formed in the late 1960s, inspired by the women's movement in the United States. This November day was the first time that the women's liberation movement was clearly recognized in Japan.

The group calling itself the Committee Preparing for Women's Liberation had distributed a pamphlet several months prior to the November forum, with the heading "An Appeal: Let's Start a Women's Liberation Movement in Japan." The writers of this pamphlet had claimed that Japanese women were oppressed in terms of both class and gender, that they were treated like "commodities in the marriage market," and that the home had been reduced to a place of escape for men, but, for women, a place "to be brainwashed by messages transmitted through television." The tract also pointed out that women were at the bottom of the employment hierarchy and were easily exploited as a reserve labor force. It further argued that sexual oppression was inseparable from Japan's imperialist colonial history as well as its on-going economic exploitation of neighboring developing countries. Therefore, the authors concluded, Japanese feminism must embrace the class struggle.

The November 14 forum lasted for seven hours and was open only to women; the 500 participants included university students, older working women, and housewives. Veteran activists, mainly leftists working in the political arena, were there as well. The Japanese news media, which had been reporting the developments of the women's liberation movement in the United States and had predicted its "landing" in Japan, called the meeting "Japan's first women's teach-in." At this time, the media coined the term *wūman ribu*, from "women's lib."

Historically, Japanese women's movements had been organized by leftist groups and labor unions, with the work carried out by a handful of women. According to the Marxist-influenced ideas of these women, women's liberation was possible only in a classless society. When it arose in Japan, *wūman ribu* presented wider-ranging propositions than had previous social and political movements in which women had been involved. Women in *wūman ribu* insisted that they did not want to wait for the arrival of the ideal; more important was to change what was wrong now. In the early 1970s, after rapid economic growth and general prosperity, both leftist and labor union movements were becoming less relevant. Nonetheless, sexual discrimination at the workplace persisted and needed to be addressed. The division of labor between husbands (who were now working longer hours) and wives (now confined in a home located farther from the city center) had become even more defined than a decade earlier. It was clear that the problems women faced were not just the result of the capitalist exploitation of workers and that those problems affected women across the spectrum of classes.

Disillusionment provoked by the sexist attitudes of some male leaders of leftist groups also attracted women to *wūman ribu*. Saitō Chiyo was one of those women. Having started her political activity in the 1960s, through the campaign against renewing the United States-Japan Security Treaty, she later helped publish a magazine, *Agora* (from the Greek word for "open space"), an important publication that provided a forum for a wide range of women. Tanaka Mitsu, who led "Group: Women Who Fight," was another such woman.

Women like Saitō and Tanaka had experienced firsthand the hypocrisy of those left-wing male liberals who supported gender equality in theory but failed to demonstrate it in practice. They also realized that women themselves had problems—a desire to please men, for instance. They recognized that many of these problems are a result of cultural conditioning, and they argued that, in the sense that they are bound by similar conditioning, all women are in the same boat. As in the United States, the Japanese women's liberation movement in its earlier stages focused on consciousness raising. Those involved in it naturally wanted to do away with the organizational hierarchy that existed in the political activities in which they had been involved. A suspicion of hierarchical structures remains a strong characteristic of the women's movement in Japan.

Like their American counterparts, Japanese women in *wūman ribu* started to examine their own internalized sexual mores and standards; they criticized their own passivity in sexual relations and tried to establish new self-images as women who could initiate rather than wait perpetually. They criticized marriage as a social institution, and a few women began to practice "free love," cohabitation, and having children outside marriage. Some women founded women's collectives in their search for an alternative lifestyle.[1]

The news media depicted the women's liberation movement at this point as a series of events concocted by a group of hyperactive women indulging in childish play, as another new fashion imported from the West; they approached the movement with a mixture of curiosity and a readiness to ridicule. By openly discussing their sexuality, some participants in *wūman ribu*, in fact, encouraged the media to interpret the movement primarily as representing a new attitude toward sex. Hence, most Japanese women did not respond or show interest in the movement at this point. One woman, for instance, recalled, in 1980, that the image she had formed of women's lib was of a movement led by young women with long, straight hair who puffed on cigarettes and looked good in their T-shirts and jeans.[2]

In the summer of 1971, a *ribu taikai*, or a women's liberation rally, was held at a mountain resort in Nagano. This retreat and rally was a *gasshuku* (a word usually associated with group training sessions for students or athletes), and it lasted for three days, with 1,200 women taking part in informal debates. The participants were encouraged to express their ideas and experiences freely. The meeting was also a women's festival, with singing, music, and a fireworks display at the closing.

According to sociologist Inoue Teruko, *ribu taikai* was a turning point in the history of the Japanese women's liberation movement.[3] After this, a greater number of women, including older women and housewives, began showing interest in participating in activities aiming at political and social changes. As a result, a wide range of new issues, such as sexism, health care delivery (particularly gynecological services), and child care became an important part of the agenda for women nationwide.

The experience of sharing among women at *ribu taikai* inspired some participants to form small local groups when they went home. For example, two women who had met on the bus on their way to Nagano started printing a nine-page newsletter called *Onnu kara onna-tachi e* ("From a Woman to Women"). Despite the fact that they lived 200 miles apart, these two women had decided to collaborate to offer a forum in which women could freely speak their minds. At its peak, the newsletter had 400 regular subscribers.

In the first week of May 1972, another *ribu taikai* was held, this time in Tokyo. With its basic theme of women's independence, it attracted more women than any previous event. "Many of us women have never thought we could be more than wives and mothers," read a leaflet inviting women to participate in the rally: "In order to become self-reliant, we must help create a society in which women can live alone if we choose to." As on previous occasions, this rally emphasized the importance of women exchanging their thoughts and experiences, but it also stressed the need for women to be united. The panel discussions featured several politically active women, including a then-prefectural assemblywoman, Ozawa Ryōko.

This 1972 rally was the springboard for *Ribu Sentā*, the Center for Women's Liberation. Established by Tanaka Mitsu and "Group: Women Who Fight," it operated from September 1972 to May 1977 in Shinjuku, Tokyo. It was run by volunteers and financed by donations and newsletter subscription fees. Among the center's activities were a round-the-clock telephone counseling service for women who had run away from home, birth control guidance, and weekly teach-ins. The center had a facility where women could stay overnight and baby-sitting services. The center also helped women form networks and groups throughout the country.

"*Ribu* Center was an attempt at a collective which would share more than physical space," Tanaka has written relating her involvement in the women's movenent; it was concerned with "women's interrelatedness."[4] Tanaka, and other women around her, believed that the goal of a woman should be to become a person who is acceptable to herself, one who is not split between what society prescribes and what she really is. The women gathered around *Ribu* Women's Center eventually dispersed into many small groups, but, throughout its operation for seven years, they adhered to their original approach of consciousness-raising as the primary means to reach liberation.

By contrast, "Women Who Fight," which emerged after the 1972 rally and carried the Japanese women's movement through the 1970s, focused its attention on political action. It first tackled the issues of birth control and abortion. Although abortion had been easily available in Japan since the end of World War II, on various grounds including "economic hardship," it was still illegal, and, during the early 1970s, the government tried to change the law to make it tougher for women to obtain the procedure. Insisting on a woman's right to reproductive choice as a prerequisite for independence and autonomy, "Women Who Fight," with mainly young career-oriented women as members, demanded no toughening of the law.

After successfully preventing the unwanted changes in the abortion law, the group embarked on other campaigns. For instance, insisting that the government lift its ban on the sale of birth control pills, the group explored ways to sell these pills outside of legal channels. It also boycotted beauty contests and sent a group of supporters to court when problematic cases of divorce, sexual discrimination, or abuse came up. The group took to the streets, wearing pink helmets in their demonstrations, and attempted to organize a women-only labor union. Because of its style of frank opposition to prevailing sexism, "Women Who Fight" received a great deal of media attention until it disbanded in 1977.

The women's journal *Agora*, mentioned above, was started in 1972. Nearly a decade earlier, its founder, Saitō, had formed the BOC (Bank of Creativity) in order to tap women's energies and focus them on social action. When this project turned out to be premature, Saitō realized that the training to see and judge for themselves was what Japanese women needed more than anything else. The publishing of *Agora*, therefore, was meant to serve as a vehicle for those who hoped to change their own consciousness before attempting to bring change in society. Supported by fourteen different groups throughout Japan, each group taking a turn at publishing it, the journal sought to provide women throughout Japan with solid information based on in-depth study and research. *Agora* has continued monthly publication for nearly two decades, and regular subscribers, mainly housewives, numbered about 800 in 1987. The members attend meetings and try to help each other improve their social awareness and self-understanding.

The effect of *Agora* on some Japanese housewives can be illustrated by the case of Takahashi Masumi.[5] She was among many women who had been involved in the care of small children and elderly parents-in-law. Suffering from a chronic shortage of sleep because of the heavy demands of caring for others, she found herself "lonely and irritable." She felt that a great deal of her life was slipping away. It had never occurred to her, though, that other women shared her feelings and frustrations or that women in other parts of the world faced similar problems.

Since she had always believed that taking care of the house and children were "jobs given to women by heaven," Takahashi was surprised when she read in *Agora* of the

United Nations declaration of the "Decade of Women" (1975–1985) and of the idea that women should share the responsibility of child rearing with men. This refreshing view made her feel better about herself—"relieved, and set her free from victim consciousness," as she put it. Takahashi decided that she should try to increase her economic self-sufficiency, while helping her husband and children learn to take care of themselves. She set as her immediate goal earning some income to finance a trip to the U.N. Women's Conference which was to be held in Copenhagen in 1980.

Takahashi attended the Copenhagen conference and afterward traveled in Norway and Sweden, where she witnessed men performing jobs traditionally assigned to women. She learned that the idea of women sharing the responsibility of child rearing with men was not so new in that part of the world. The sense of solidarity with women elsewhere encouraged Takahashi to go on attempting to bring changes in her life.

When the U.N. Conference on Women was held in Nairobi five years later, in 1985, a large number of Japanese women participated, and some of them held workshops. One headed by Tamura Katsuko, a manager of a supermarket, reported on the circumstances of Japanese part-time women workers, including the low pay and poor job security. Even in labor unions with more women members than men, Tamura reported, the officers were almost always men.[6] Tamura's report puzzled many delegates from other countries at the workshop. Women in developing countries, who had expected to hear how Japanese women were benefiting from their country's economic success, concluded that Japan did not set a good example for women in developing countries and that a highly developed economy does not necessarily benefit women, Tamura reported.

The declaration of the Decade of Women also helped energize Japanese women who believed in direct social and political action. It triggered, for example, a new group formed by several politically active women, including Ichikawa Fusae, a veteran member of the Diet, and prefectural assemblywoman Ozawa Ryōko. First, this group voiced its objection to the government-picked delegation to a 1975 U.N. Conference in Mexico (which initiated the Women's Decade), maintaining that the delegation did not well represent Japanese women. Later, collecting signatures and organizing women's meetings, this group protested discriminatory practices in the media, education, and politics. By supporting a number of legal actions taken by women, they also tried to make discrimination against women in the workplace better known to the public.

The group continued its activities after the U.N. Women's Decade ended in 1985. Having changed its name to "Women Who Bring Action," it extended its areas of interest and formed various subgroups, focusing even on such issues as pornography and feminist theory. One subgroup called "Network Sisters" helped to develop connections among many diverse women's groups throughout the country.

Through the activities of these various groups and others, the women's movement was brought closer to the daily lives of ordinary women in Japan. In the spring of 1993, the production of a documentary film titled "From Women to Women" was underway. It tells the stories of six women on the front lines of *wūman ribu* during the 1970s and records an important but now virtually forgotten page of history.[7] Kurihara Nakako, who interviewed the six women, including Tanaka Mitsu, and put archival photographs and footage together to produce the documentary, stated how shocked she was to discover the distorted way the news media at large had reported on the women's liberation movement of the 1970s. Having found that these women had not only survived but were living independent lives with their original convictions intact, Kurihara found her role models in them. There has been considerable improvement in media reporting on feminist activities in recent years, partially because of an increase in the number of women reporters.

Exposing sexism in its various forms had been one of the most recent focuses of Japanese feminists. "A Network of Women Concerned with Sexual Harassment in the Workplace" was organized in 1989 and is led by a group of women attorneys. The group conducted a survey in July of that year and discovered that more than half of sexual harassment victims—all women—were either fired or resigned as the result of refusing to go along with their bosses' advances. The Tokyo Association of Women Attorneys held a telephone counseling session one day in October 1989; 138 callers, including a few men, related incidents of sexual harassment, mostly sexual advances by immediate superiors.[8] *Onna no union Kanagawa*, a fifty-member union established in 1990 to try and solve problems encountered by women in their workplaces, has successfully settled fourteen cases of sexual harassment.[9] There is also an organization of academic women formed in support of a young woman harassed by her mentor, a prominent scholar, in 1994.

The issue of sexual harassment started to draw public interest in Japan around 1989 and was quickly picked up by the media.[10] The industrial sector and government have responded, conducting surveys,[11] studying cases in both Japan and the United States, and distributing a manual with the intent of preventing harassment. Many Japanese men find the concept of sexual harassment extremely hard to grasp.[12] Having been used to mixing work with social activities and being pampered by hostesses at bars and nightclubs, they are quite puzzled at the recent developments that indict their seemingly "normal" behavior. But women are learning that they do not have to take insults.

In the spring of 1987, when I was living in Japan, I came across a book entitled *Onna no netowākingu* (*Women's Networking*, by Hisada Kei, 1987). A 300-page book, it lists various types of organizations and thus gives a rough idea of the scope of women's social and other group activities in Japan during the past few decades.

Thirty different groups are listed in the "women's history" section of *Women's Networking*, and some of these groups hold nationwide meetings. Apparently, the participants in these meetings often go beyond the study of traditional history and exchange their experiences of, for example, the sexual discrimination encountered in their daily lives, in a kind of oral history. At the meeting in Hokkaidō, for example, Okinawa women talked about their experiences during World War II, comparing notes with women of the Ainu, a small minority group in Hokkaidō. These women were in fact interested in both the process of self-discovery as well as history. In this sense, their activities, although they might not be called "feminist," were definitely a part of the larger social movement of Japanese women that started in the 1970s.

The peace movement has always had a strong appeal for Japanese women. Since the 1960s, various women's organizations have worked for a decrease in the military budget. *Deruta* (Delta), a women's group in Hiroshima listed in the above-mentioned book, collected testimony from *hibakusha*, A-bomb victims; women in the cities with U.S. military bases have also organized themselves to press for nuclear disarmament. Some of these women have made contacts with women working for the same goal in Greenham Common, in England. Other groups—"Women Blocking the Passage to War," for example—were formed during the early 1980s in reaction to the shift to the right within the Liberal Democratic Party and a fear of renewed militarism.

There are also women's groups that work to expose the exploitation by Japanese men of young women from the Third World, mainly the Philippines and Thailand. Recruited by organized crime syndicates, the *yakuza*, to work at bars and nightclubs, these women, lured by the promise of high wages, are often forced into prostitution. An estimated 4 to 5 million of these women were living in Japan in 1987.[13] The women's groups also work to expose the practice of Japanese businessmen visiting Asian countries on "sex tours," which are sightseeing visits that include the services of prostitutes.

One evening in the winter of 1988, I attended a meeting of a group interested in this issue, the Japanese branch of the Asian Women's Research and Action Network (AWRAN), which was formed in 1982. "We've got to make Japanese wives realize that it is they who allow their husbands to go to Southeast Asia on sex tours," said one woman at the meeting held at the Kyoto YWCA. In protesting the tours, Japanese women's groups have cooperated with women's groups in Korea and Taiwan, conducting studies on how these tours are organized and operated.

In the field of education, a group of women collected funds to support a magazine, *Atarashii Kateika Ui* (*New Course on Home Economics: "We"*). Its publisher, Handa Tatsuko, is a veteran textbook editor; the women who backed her held the position that the high school curriculum policy should be changed to make home economics compulsory for boys as well as girls. They hoped that acquiring basic domestic skills at high school age would make Japanese husbands more self-sufficient and more willing to share household responsibility with their wives. Even more importantly, they objected to existing national policy because it reflected the sexism and gender inequality permeating home and society.

During the 1980s, a handful of Japanese feminists also targeted the sexism permeating primary and secondary school textbooks and other teaching materials. Conducting my own research in 1987, I found their objections to be well founded. In one first-grade textbook, for example, I found pictures of a mother preparing breakfast and helping a child to dress, while the father reads a newspaper. The accompanying questions ask: "What does Masao's mother do to help the family?" and "Who does the shopping?" In another section, called "Family Life and Money," the book asked: "Who works and earns money to support your family?" These questions encourage the notion of rigid gender role division. Both historical and contemporary figures appearing in the officially approved textbooks were mostly men. An examination of social studies textbooks showed that, out of twenty biographies, only one was about a woman, Marie Curie; the rest were entirely about men.[14]

In addition to organizations that parallel to many found in the United States—the Parent Teacher Association, the League of Women Voters, and women's sections in the major political parties—Japanese women have, since the end of World War II, developed a few large-scale national organizations of their own. The National Council of Women's Organization of Agricultural Cooperatives is a well-organized body, and the National Federation of Regional Women's Organizations has a membership of over 20,000 regional women's groups; the Housewives Association also has branches all over the country. These groups have taken an interest primarily in issues involving consumer protection, environmental quality, and peace.

With memberships ranging from a dozen to a few hundred, diverse groups of women listed in *Women's Networking* serve different types of needs. Rather than attending large-scale rallies and demonstrations, individual women choose specific areas of interest and form small groups. Although limited in their political effectiveness, such groups are easy to form, and the members have the advantage of being involved in activities based on neighborhood and community ties.

Many of the changes that have taken place during the past few decades have affected Japanese women both directly and indirectly, and the women want to understand these changes. By 1975, increasing numbers of Japanese housewives were questioning the traditional roles that tied them to their homes; they also became worried about caring for elderly parents and preparing for their own old age. These women were and are realizing that there is more than one way of living. Through the various groups in which they actively participate, they are not only learning about issues that affect them but are also being trained how to think and judge on their own.

9

Women and Political Power

In July 1989, it was reported that the Japanese Socialist Party's victory in the Upper House election was due largely to the power of women. Some of my American friends asked me if this reflected a radical change in the status of women in Japan and if it was really a "revolution," as some newspaper articles had put it. In Tokyo, Shimomura Mitsuko, a veteran reporter for the *Asahi Shimbun*, stated that, for a few weeks after the news was released, she received numerous telephone calls from foreign correspondents asking the same question.[1]

It is indeed a challenge to explain this sudden burst of interest in politics among Japanese women, which resulted in an "upset" election. The so-called "geisha scandal"—public disclosures about the paid mistress of newly chosen Prime Minister Uno Sōsuke, leader of the perpetually ruling Liberal Democratic Party (LDP)—did not seem an adequate explanation.[2] Even the *Rikurūto* ("recruit") scandal, in which bribery proved to be more widespread than Japanese voters had imagined, was not the whole story.

Lacking a single specific answer to my friends' questions, I was able to respond only that Japanese women have shown an increasing interest in making both personal and social changes in recent years. Shimomura has similarly asserted that Japanese women had been preparing for this political victory for a decade or so. Shimomura has also maintained that, although the women's movement in Japan had not been as widespread and visible as that in the United States, changes in the social and personal awareness of Japanese women, particularly since 1975, were significant. Only Japanese men, including her male colleagues, she said, had not observed this.

The history of Japanese women's participation in politics is barely a half-century old (while the national Diet has existed for slightly more than one century).[3] In the first general election under universal suffrage, held in April 1946, seventy-nine women candidates ran and thirty-six were elected, making up 8.9 percent of the Lower House representatives; 67 percent of eligible women voters cast their ballots (not far below the 78.5 percent for men) at that time. Contrary to general skepticism expressed, particularly by male politicians, Japanese women showed a keen interest in their new opportunity for political involvement. The gap between the voting rates of men and women has continued to close, and, since 1968, more women have voted than men, making Japan one of the few countries in the world where women outvote men. There has never been a larger number of women candidates elected in a national election since, however, and, for a long time, the proportion of women in the legislature has remained around 3 percent (1 percent in the Upper House). The political representation of women at the national level has not kept pace with the advances Japanese women have made in business, academia, and other professional fields.[4]

As mentioned above, the number of women representatives in the Diet sharply increased (from 3 to 13 percent) in

1989; this was the result of the 1989 Upper House elections, primarily the victory of the Japanese Socialist Party (JSP). There had been several other cases in which women candidates, backed by this party, had won victories. For example, earlier the same year, a woman beat her male opponent by a large margin in the by-election for the Prefectural Assembly in Niigata, a conservative region in northern Japan. This was a totally unexpected victory for "a mere housewife" over an experienced and influential male politician. In the important election for the Tokyo Metropolitan Assembly (in July 1989), the JSP tripled its number of seats. As a result of this election, seventeen women (of a total of thirty-three women candidates) were elected to office; of the twelve winners whom the Socialist Party backed, nine were newcomers to politics. Not only observers abroad but also Japanese themselves asked "Why." While men in general saw the change as a fluke, many women perceived it as the result of a major structural shift in Japanese politics.

The JSP, Japan's second-largest party had once, in 1958, occupied 35.5 percent of the seats in the House of Representatives and had participated, in 1947, in a coalition government. Nonetheless, it had gained by then a negative image as the party that said "no" to everything. One might naturally wonder, then, if all of these 1989 victories were thanks to the successful leadership of Doi Takako, then the leader of the party. Doi, a former teacher and constitutional scholar, took her leadership position in the party in the aftermath of a major defeat in the elections of the Upper House in 1986. Although she was chosen despite some objections from influential party members (who felt that a woman would not be able to direct the party), she succeeded in revamping the party's negative image. Her vitality made her a symbol of the JSP's effort to take a new direction.[5] The time was also right for her. Signs of corruption in an "old-boy" network, as well as the self-complacency and arrogance among LDP Diet members, had greatly affronted Japanese voters, particularly women, who were also angered by the introduction of a national consumption tax. New developments on the international scene, particularly the weakened East-West tensions, had reduced concerns about some of the JSP's foreign policies. The ruling LDP lost twenty seats in the Diet at the 1989 election.

Supporting women candidates and uniting them in opposition to the LDP has been Doi's famous "Madonna strategy."[6] Under her leadership, the JSP urged women who were local leaders in such groups as the PTA and consumer cooperatives to run for office. As a result, the 1989 Tokyo Metropolitan Assembly election, already mentioned, fielded more women candidates than any other election in the history of Tokyo, and the news media described the great success of women candidates in various elections that year as the "Madonna cyclone that shook Japan."[7]

The Madonna strategy, however, was not totally a new idea.[8] Feminist groups such as "Women Who Bring Action" (see Chapter 7) had been aware of the potential political power of women and had sponsored meetings where representatives of women's organizations discussed how to encourage women to run for office and how to help them address the issues important to them—discrimination in the workplace, the environment, education, and care for the aged. Throughout the 1980s, in fact, an increasing number of Japanese women had shown their understanding that, through political processes, they would be able to help solve the problems confronting them and their families. During the past decade, Japanese women (who generally do better in school than men but find far fewer significant roles in society after their graduation) have been encouraged by the growing female consciousness.[9]

That women can be particularly effective in single-issue elections had already been shown in Zushi, a suburb of Tokyo, where, in 1982, the residents organized themselves in opposition to the construction of housing for U.S. military personnel stationed in nearby Yokosuka. The majority of participants in this citizens' group were women, and they succeeded in recalling the mayor. Through this process (which the media called "an experiment in democracy"), many women in Zushi learned the principles of self-governance. Five years later, in 1987, women in Zushi were among those throughout Japan who demonstrated their political clout in the election of various local assemblies. The fifty-two women elected at this time, ranging in age from twenty-six to seventy-four, were all newcomers to politics and were supported by various women's organizations.

The endorsement of women candidates with few political ties, such as Yanagitani Akiko, characterized many elections in the 1980s. Yanagitani, a nursery school teacher and an active member of "A Group For Autonomous Citizens," was persuaded by the city's JSP-backed mayor to run for the city assembly in Fujisawa. Her election slogan was "Change the World from the Kitchen," and her campaign workers were mostly housewives. Divorced and with two children, Yanagitani supported herself and her family on unemployment benefits and a loan during the campaign. She amazed her opponent by showing that one can win an election with very little money.

It is certain that the electoral successes of women candidates paved the way for Moriyama Mayumi and Takahara Sumiko to take important governmental positions in 1989. With a more subdued personality than Doi, Moriyama had had a long career in government, including posts as Director of the Women's and Young Workers' Bureau, Parliamentary Vice-Minister for Foreign Affairs, and Minister for the Environment Agency, before she was appointed Chief Cabinet Secretary, a post with great influence that had traditionally been filled by a senior politician (the person who holds this post is generally considered the prime minister's right-hand "man").[10] Takahara, an economic commentator, accepted the post of Minister of State for the Economic Planning Agency, also in 1989. Her first job was to tone down the harsh anti-LDP criticism over the consumption tax and to deal with U.S. Trade Representative Carla Hills, whose hard-line attitude toward Japan was well known. The LDP, which had lost the 1989 Upper House election by failing to get the women's vote, clearly elevated these two women to high posts in an effort to appeal to women voters and also in order to project a "clean" image, particularly after the sex scandals. Five years earlier, no one could have imagined an Upper House Budget Committee meeting with two women sitting in the cabinet minister seats, facing old and new female Diet members—representatives of the "Madonnas"—in the front rows.[11]

A journalist friend who was visiting me from Japan in the fall of 1989 was not very optimistic about the political influence of Doi Takako. Doi, who had had little involvement in party politics previously, has been criticized by the left wing within the JSP because she has no clear strategy for taking power; she also seems not to be very good at coordinating her membership. In October 1989, a JSP-backed woman candidate lost a seat to an LDP candidate in a by-election in Ibaraki prefecture. The *Yomiuri Shimbun*'s survey at the end of the same month showed that support for the JSP had dropped (from 42.9 percent in July to 22.7 percent in October). Its unconvincing substitute measures to replace the consumption tax and the so-called "pachinko scandal" (the JSP allegedly accepted political contributions from the General Association of Korean Residents in Japan, which is involved in running many pachinko parlors), were the immediate causes of this rapid decline in popularity.

More criticisms were directed at Doi herself. Among these was her unwillingness to reach out for support beyond grass-roots groups of feminists, environmentalists and other political activists.[12] Unable to come up with viable strategies to take power or overcome factional differences, in May

1991, Doi left her position as the first woman party head in Japan. Her chairmanship was reportedly conceived as a temporary one.[13] The JSP continued to lose the confidence of Japanese voters, and in a House of Representatives election in July 1993, the party lost nearly half of the 134 seats it had held.

Nonetheless, the number of women who came to understand that grass-roots activisim could be an effective means to express their political choices did not decrease with the defeat of their symbolic leader, Doi Takako. At the end of 1991, for the first time in Japanese history, three women were elected as vice-governors in Tokyo, Okinawa, and Ishikawa prefectures. The nation's first woman mayor (in Ashiya, Hyogo Prefecture) was also elected in 1991. In February 1992, a National Federation of Feminist Representatives was formed, with the goal of securing 30 percent of representation in national, prefectural, and other local assemblies. In July 1992, an Upper House election showed an increase in women elected. Still, the number (thirty-seven) was disproportionately small. The rates of women represented in the Lower House and in local assemblies, 2.4 percent and 3.2 percent, respectively, are even smaller.

Most Japanese women's traditional perception of their gender role does not include political participation. More so than men, women have seen national politics as a realm of power plays and buying influence, a filthy world that has nothing to do with their lives and values. They tend to be interested in a limited range of issues, such as consumer rights or health and environmental concerns.[14] On the national level of politics, women continue to remain ineffective against the scandal-ridden union between big business and the government.

In July 1993, however, the LDP's thirty-eight years of majority rule ended. In that month's House of Representatives election, as many as seventy women candidates ran (the largest field since 1955, when the LDP took power) and fourteen of them were elected. Among them were Koike Yuriko, who had run on the ticket of the Japan New Party, a party formed immediately before the general election that year by former members of the LDP. Tanaka Makiko, the eldest daughter of Tanaka Kakuei (the former prime minister who had been forced to resign because of his involvement in the Lockheed scandal), ran as an independent and captured her father's electorate. Doi Takako also won in this election, and, when a coalition government was formed with Hosokawa Morihiro as the head, she became the first woman to serve as speaker. Other new faces were Takaichi Sanae, a political commentator in her thirties from Nara Prefecture, who won without the backing of any political party; a television commentator, Ito Hideko, and a television announcer, Okazaki Tomiko, from the northern prefecture of Miyagi. Ishida Mie, an independent, was the first woman representative to the House of Representatives from Okayama Prefecture in forty-one years.[15]

According to a 1987 Prime Minister's Office survey, more than two-thirds of the women respondents who were in their thirties, compared to only 20 percent of those in their sixties, felt that more women should be involved in politics. The most recent general election has also shown that a growing number of younger women candidates want to extend their managerial or executive skills, which they have acquired in the workplace, into political action. As women continue to achieve higher status in their jobs, their interest and savvy in the social and political arenas is expected to increase as well. In the 1993 election, 33 million women (3 million more than men) cast their ballots, showing their strong interest in political processes, at least partly as a result of grass-roots campaigns and the educational efforts of many women's groups. Furthermore, many women are now casting their votes with the clear intention of bringing about changes, rather than out of a sense of duty or under the influence of their husbands and male acquaintances. As Shimomura has stated, Japanese women in general have become more conscious of their political power during the 1980s. There is no reason to believe that they will lose this raised consciousness any time soon.

Notes

Note: All publishers are located in Tokyo unless otherwise indicated. Japanese names in both the notes and the main text have been written using the Japanese convention of "last name first," that is to say, family name followed by personal name.

INTRODUCTION

1. Most of this increase was concentrated in three areas: Tokyo, Osaka, and Nagoya. In 1962, Tokyo became the largest city in the world, with a population approaching 10 million.

2. Both white- and blue-collar workers put in long hours, as many as 202.7 hours a month (a 1960 figure). They slowly reduced their hours toward the end of the 1960s, but, around 1975, they went back to the old pattern of long working hours.

3. Tsuda College was founded in 1900 by Tsuda Umeko, a woman who was sent to the United States at age six, raised by an American couple, and educated at Bryn Mawr; the college enjoyed generous financial support from Tsuda's American friends. Even at the time I was a student, there were several teachers who, following the founder's example, conducted their classes in English.

4. Exchange rates given throughout the text are approximate and vary according to the time period.

CHAPTER 1

1. The initial draft, prepared by U.S. Occupation officials, stated that "marriage shall be founded upon mutual consent instead of parental coercion, and maintained through cooperation instead of male domination." Some Japanese, including Satō Kenji, a political scientist, maintain that there is a significant difference between the two versions: by implicitly ruling out parental interference ("*only* on . . . mutual consent") rather than merely prohibiting parental coercion, Satō has stated, the constitution deemed that all marriage must be love marriage. The underlying logic of the constitution, therefore, is that love may require defiance of one's parents. "People Who Can Only Play at Love," *Japan Quarterly* (Winter 1993).

2. Although most of my friends in high school expressed a preference for *ren'ai* marriage, quite a few of them ended up married via *miai* arrangements.

3. The number of nuclear families started to climb around 1960. The same amount of flurry around royal nuptials was not seen thirty-five years later, when current Crown Prince Naruhito married Masako Ōwada, a U.S.-educated career diplomat. Japanese businesses hoped in vain for a repeat of the huge extent of consumer activity and television viewing during 1993.

4. Population Study Institute, Ministry of Health and Welfare. In contrast, more than three-quarters of the marriages surveyed in the mid-1950s were considered *miai* marriages. As for preferences between *ren'ai* and *miai* marriages, this survey found that more women than men in general considered *ren'ai* desirable; the younger the respondent, the stronger the preference for *ren'ai*, while almost none (fewer than 2 percent) considered *miai* a preferable form. Acceptance of *miai* (in the form of an "either way" response) increased with age.

5. In another survey, done in 1990, the top three were: "being able to talk together about feelings," followed by "being in love," and "financial security," with a very small difference between the second and the third. This study compared the ratings with those among American women, for whom the important considerations were "being in love," "sexual fidelity on the part of spouse," and "being able to talk about feelings." Iwao Sumiko, *The Japanese Woman* (New York: Free Press, 1993), 70.

6. "Advice to the Lonely: Marriage is Self-Affirmation," *Japan Echo* (Special Issue, 1988).

7. *Seimeihoken bunka sentā, Hachijūnendai no josei no seikatsu: genzai to shōrai* [*Women's Lives in the 80s: Present and Future*] (Nihon Hōsō Shuppan kyōkai, 1983), 78.

8. In Yuzawa, Akita Prefecture, the number of unmarried men over age thirty also doubled in the decade from 1975 to 1985. One farmer reportedly stated that the question of liberalizing imports of U.S. agricultural products was a less urgent matter. *Japan Quarterly* (July-September, 1988). Also *Asahi Shimbun* (3–12 March 1988).

9. According to Itamoto Yōko, the head of a marriage agency and author of the book, *Gendai Kekkon Jijō* [*Contemporary Scenes of Marriages*] (Ie no Hikari Association, 1987) the total enrollment of these agencies is nearly 200,000, with an annual profit of 200 million yen ($1.5 million). It is the opinion of Satō Noriko of Japan BMS, a marriage agency, that men, even more than women, want to settle down and that this might be a sign that men in their late twenties and thirties feel that opportunities for getting ahead in the corporate world are steadily diminishing; they want to retreat into the private world of marriage. Unlike men of older generations, young men today also do not believe that successes as a company man is the most important goal in life. *Asahi Jānaru* [*Asahi Journal*] (16 October 1987).

10. *Kōbe Shimbun* (5 April 1984).

11. A survey administered to male Chūō University students, for example, found that the four most common reasons for men to marry are to have children, to be with the woman one loves, the momentum of circumstance, and parental expectations. *Kōbe Shimbun* (30 May 1984).

12. Joseigaku kenkyū kai (Association of Women's Studies), *Kōza: Joseigaku* [*Lectures on Women's Studies*], vol. 2, (Keisōshobō, 1984), 80–82.

13. Kamiko Takeji, *Nihon no Kazokukankei* [*Family Dynamics in Japan*] (Yūhikaku, 1981), 64.

14. A closer look at financial decisions made by Japanese couples reveals the limitations on a Japanese wife's power, however. Decisions on a major purchase such as a house, for instance, are much more frequently made by the husband alone than by the wife alone (35.5 percent versus 2.1 percent, in one survey). *Women's Lives in the 80s*, p. 80.

15. Kamiko, *Family Dynamics*, 66.

16. Prime Minister's Office Survey, "Equality between Men and Women." The figure, however, shows a decrease in the number of people who support these gender roles, by nearly 15 percent among women surveyed in 1979. *Nihon Keizai Shimbun* (23 March 1993).

17. Until recently, single women in Japan found it extremely hard to obtain mortgage loans; a friend of mine, a professional woman in her late forties, had to present her case on an application as though she needed a house to enable her mother, her dependent, to live with her.

18. *Japan Quarterly* (July–September 1987).

19. Although the current law, unlike the old pre-World War II civil codes, allows couples to choose either of their surnames, new couples almost always choose the name of the husband.

20. Some people would go so far as to say that the current registry system is based on the civil codes of 1887 and that it has remained intact for a specific reason, beyond administrative considerations: to discourage people from having children outside of marriage. Inoue Haruyo, *Josei no sei o kaeshite* [*Give Us Back Our Names*] (Osaka: Sōgensha, 1986).

21. This law reveals the Japanese view of marriage as a family matter: Divorce severs a woman's tie to her in-law's family, so her surname must be changed back to her maiden name. A change made in 1976, allowing women to retain their names after divorce by making a request to that effect within three months, has made divorce logistically less cumbersome. In particular, it has minimized the adverse effects upon career women, for whom a name change can be professionally damaging.

CHAPTER 2

1. *Kōbe Shimbun* (5 May 1985).

2. Japan's recent economic recession has made steady promotion, even for loyal employees, difficult; it has even forced the demoting or firing of some. As a result, more "corporate soldiers" have begun questioning their sense of loyalty to their companies, some opting to spend more time with their families.

3. Japanese drinkers had always been mostly male, and they consumed alcohol mainly to lose their inhibitions. Now, with the help of increased individual disposable income and a concerted marketing effort by the alcoholic beverage industry, the ratio of female to male drinkers in the Japanese population has reached the European level: 1.0 woman to 1.4 men. *Japan Quarterly* 33: 1 (1986).

4. The first excerpts from this study were published in *Kōbe Shimbun* (6 April 1983), and later in *Nihonjin no sei* [*The Japanese and Sex*] (Bungei Shunjūsha, 1984). Quotes are from *Kōbe Shimbun*.

5. Ibid.

6. David W. Plath et al., eds., *Work and Lifecourse in Japan* (Albany, NY: State University of New York Press, 1983), 201.

7. *Kōbe Shimbun* (6 April 1983).

8. While problems such as a lack of adequate space to raise children and the high cost of education can be considered "economic reasons," little attention has been given to the issue of women's right to choose.

9. Because her husband's transfer to Saudi Arabia meant she would be separated from him for five years, one wife decided to protest, but, when she tried to enlist support from other employees' wives, she met with considerable discouragement. "Since he comes back once in a while, it isn't so bad," they told her. *Asahi Jānaru* (30 November 1987).

10. Ibid.

11. For further analysis of "Falling in Love," see *Japan Quarterly* 33: 2 (1986).

12. *Seimeihoken bunka sentā, Hachijūnendai no josei no seikatsu: genzai to shōrai* [*Women's Lives in the 80s: Present and Future*] (Nihon Hōsō Shuppan kyōkai, 1983), 30.

13. *Asahi Jānaru* (16 November 1984).

CHAPTER 3

1. In the period since the end of World War II, the Japanese divorce rate dropped to its lowest point around 1962, with a total number of about 70,000 a year.

2. Fewer Japanese women now believe their sole destiny is to be a wife and mother; this belief goes along with the sentiment that self-sacrifice and the capacity to endure in marriage are no longer womanly virtues.

3. *Seimeihoken bunka sentā, Hachijūnendai no josei no seikatsu* [*Women's Lives in the 80s*] (Nihon Hōsō Shuppan kyōkai, 1983), 114–16.

4. *Bungeishunjū* [*Literary Seasons*] (April 1989).

5. Sakamoto Fuyuko, *Josei no kenri* [*Women's Rights*] (Hōritsu bunkasha, 1982), 55.

6. *Kōbe Shimbun* (27 July 1983).

7. *Women's Lives in the 80s.*

8. *Fujin Kōron* (July 1984).

9. *Kōbe Shimbun* (4 May 1984).

10. When it reversed its previous decision, the court carefully stipulated that the divorce was granted because no minor children were involved and because the financial circumstances of the party being divorced were sound.

11. The case is from Sawachi Hisae, *Ai ga sabakareru toki* [*When Love Is on Trial*], (Bungeishunjū, 1983).

12. Sakamoto, p. 57.

13. *Asahi Shimbun* (29 August 1987).

14. The special considerations for widows may have been related to the fact that Japan had been used to giving special treatment to war widows.

CHAPTER 4

1. The number of nuclear households increased from 62 percent in 1955 to 68.2 percent in 1965.

2. This was seen, for example, in newspaper columns such as the readers' contribution sections and in letters. Amano Masako, "Gendai nihon no hahaoya kan" ["Images of Mothers in Modern Japan"], *Joseigaku kenkyū kai, Kōza Joseigaku [Lectures on Women's Studies]*, vol. 1 (Keisōshobō, 1984), 79, 80.

3. One article was titled "Gauging Mothers' Intent for Murder." During the first ten months of 1969, there had been twenty-nine infanticides known to the police. *Amano*, 81.

4. Akatsuka Yukio, *Sengo yokubō shi* [*Post-War History of Desire*], vol. 3 (Kōdansha, 1985), 96.

5. One social critic, Adachi Wakako, who had come to realize that instances of mothers trying to murder their children were not isolated occurrences, helped form a support group of mothers, which straightforwardly called itself "Women Who Are Concerned about Child-Killing." *Jinsie dokuhon: hahaoya [A Book on Life: Motherhood]* (Kawade shobō, 1981), 67.

6. *Seimeihoken bunka sentā, Hachijūnendai no josei no seikatsu: genzai to shōrai*, 11.

7. Ibid., 10.

8. *Fujin Kōron* (Special Issue, 1981).

9. Edwin O. Reischauer, *The Japanese* (Cambridge, MA: Harvard University Press, 1982), 172.

10. Even though 97 percent of children now attend high school—compared to 50 percent in my day, some thirty years ago—high school education in Japan is not compulsory, and entrance exams are required to attend. Furthermore, one has to attend the right high school in order to do well on university entrance exams. Admission to these schools, many of which are private, has become very competitive during the past

few decades. The ordeal of studying for an entrance exam, "examination hell," used to begin in the last year of high school. Pressure has escalated in the past decade, however, and now competition starts even before the child enters middle school.

11. Japanese mothers' emphasis on effort goes along with a general belief among Japanese that much of the reward exists in the effort itself. Since failure is perceived as related not so much to innate ability as to effort, it is all the more psychologically devastating to fail an entrance examination. In this light, it is interesting to note that a study conducted by the University of Michigan found that only 40 percent of Japanese mothers were satisfied with their children's schools, while the majority of American mothers considered their children's schools to be either good or excellent. The University of Michigan study was originally reported in the *New York Times* and later reprinted in *Kōbe Shimbun* (18 June 1984).

12. "Nippon hōsō shuppan kyōkai, Zenkoku chōsa: Katei to kyōiku" ["A Nationwide Survey by the Japan Broadcasting Association, 'Family and Education,'" *Hachijūnendai josei no seikatsu: genzai to shōrai* [*Life in the 80s: Present and Future*], 51.

13. Although strong parental interest and participation are frequently referred to as key to success in Japanese education, little attention has been paid to gender differences in parental expectations. My friend Akiko commented on this difference as she had observed it in parents. Mothers of boys, she says, are much more serious about college entrance examinations. On the other hand, many Japanese parents see their daughter's goal as a happy marriage; higher education for her is primarily a means to find a job in case she has to support herself for some unforeseen reason. Women often select two-year college degrees in practical fields such as nursing and child care. Interestingly, it is frequently mothers, rather than fathers, who espouse different treatments for their sons and daughters with regard to college education. One survey showed that, while 334 out of 1,000 male high school seniors went to four-year colleges in 1985 and 1986, only 123 out of 1,000 female seniors did; only 27 male, in contrast to 177 female, students opted to attend two-year institutions. Ministry of Education (1989).

14. *Kōbe Shimbun* (24 December 1983).

15. *Nippon hōsō shuppan kyōkai, Zenkoku chōsa: Nihonjin no ishiki* [*A Nation-wide Survey: Perceptions of the Japanese*] (Nippon hōsō kyōkai shuppan, 1983), 50. The survey was done in 1978.

CHAPTER 5

1. *Kicchin* was made into a film in Japan; when its English translation was published in the United States (New York: Washington Square Press, 1993), it also made the best-seller list.

2. "A Kinder, Gentler Generation," *Look Japan* (April 1991). The survey, conducted in 1985, had 3,600 male and female respondents ages thirteen to twenty-nine, throughout Japan. Also see *Nippon no wakamono* [*Japan's Youth*] (Nippon Hōsō Shuppan Kyōkai, 1986) and Nakano Osamu, "Shinjinrui Genron," *Seiron* (November 1986).

3. "Rōjn no seikatsu to ishiki: Kokusai hikaku chōsa kekka hōkoku" ("Life and Opinions of the Elderly: Report on Comparative Studies"), Prime Minister's Office, 1988.

4. *Hanako*, started at the height of Japan's economic "bubble," contains stock market listings, horse race results, and information on where to find "hot," chic 50,000-yen-a-night Ginza hotels, among other things. Lifestyles change at a nontraditional pace in publications like *Hanako*. It once described women who have children as *bakabakashii* (foolish) but later, following the "Kiko boom" (when young Princess Kiko gave birth), advocated *Okāsan de ganbarō!* ("Let's go with motherhood!"). *Japan Times* (16 July 1992).

5. According to a *Yomiuri Shimbun* opinion poll of young men and women in their twenties, 81 percent said they would change jobs, as opposed to 51 percent of people in their fifties. See also *Look Japan* (April 1991). Young people tend to switch jobs easily, says Shimojū, because, unlike a few decades ago, opportunities to find different forms of employment—part-time, free-lancing, temporary, etc.—are much greater now.

6. "People Who Can Only Play at Love," *Japan Echo* (Winter, 1993).

7. *Japan Quarterly* 33, no. 1 (1986).

8. *Japan Echo* (2 November 1989).

9. *Kōbe Shimbun* (30 May 1984).

10. *Bungeishunjū* (April 1989).

11. *Japan Echo* (Spring 1989).

12. *Look Japan* (April 1991).

13. The underground popularity of girls' comics has existed since the mid-1970s. There were several monthly and weekly girls' magazines then, selling nearly 200 million copies per month. The influence of these comics can be seen in the work of Yoshimoto Banana. According to social critic Inukai Tomoko, who says that she herself was an avid reader of these comics, their popularity was largely ignored because what inter-

ests teenage girls is generally considered unimportant. *Bessatsu Takarajima* 4 (1977).

14. "The New Generation Gap," *Atlantic Monthly* (December 1992).

15. *Kōseishō* (Ministry of Health and Welfare), *Seishōnen Hakusho*, [*White Paper on Youth*] (1987).

16. *Japan Quarterly*, a publication of the Consulate-General Office of Seattle (January–March 1990).

17. Hayashi Masayuki, *Hikōshōjo to yobu maeni* [*Before You Call Them Delinquent Girls*], (Hihyōsha, 1981), 190.

18. *Fujin Kōron* (March 1975).

19. Akatsuka Yukio, *Sengo yokubōshi* [*Post-War History of Desire*], vol. 2, (Kōdansha, 1985), 115–17.

20. Hayashi, 70–71.

21. Ibid., 73.

22. The most recent invention by the "pink industry" that I have come across is *sekuhara bā* (sexual harassment bar), in which a woman in a provocative dress with a word processor on her lap is presented to the customers. *Nyūsuwīku* [Japanese edition of *Newsweek*] (31 October 1991).

23. Although Turkish baths changed their name to "soaplands," local citizens' groups successfully passed ordinances to get rid of them, resulting in more discreet operations such as "date clubs," "lovers' banks," and *mantoru* (soaplands operated in a "mansion," or condominium). Call-girl systems, in which women are dispatched to a client's hotel room, are also now a major source of income for the *yakuza*, who function as pimps.

24. For over 300 years, prostitution had been a government-regulated, taxed, and lucrative business in Japan. As a result of the 1956 law, which was a major victory for numerous women's and other groups who had pushed for reform for over half a century, 130,000 prostitutes nationwide were put out of work. *Japan Quarterly* (January–March 1988).

25. *Fujin Kōron* (June 1985).

26. For more information, see *Sekai* (July 1993).

27. *Pop-Teens* is unique among the various magazines for teenage girls, in that it includes articles beyond those featuring movie stars, fashion, and interior design. It discusses sexual intercourse, the biology of pregnancy, birth control, and abortion. *Fujin Kōron* (August 1982).

28. *Kōbe Shimbun* (23 April 1985).

29. *Fujin Kōron* (June 1986).

30. Hayashi, 118.

31. Japan seems to have a fad for converting everything into comic book form, from classical literature to rape; a comic series *Za reipuman* [*The Rape-Man*] was made into a thirteen-volume book set after being serialized in a man's magazine. In addition, there is a computer game in which a female body is cut up and eventually raped.

32. A 1979 *Keishichō* (National Police Headquarters) survey.

33. Hayashi, 133.

34. *Asahi Jānaru* (8 September 1989).

CHAPTER 6

1. Rōdōshō (Ministry of Labor), *Fujin rōdō no jitsujyō* ("State of Female Labor Force," 1982).

2. Sugawara Mariko, *Josei Kanrishoku no jidai* [*The Era of Female Managers*] (Chikuma Shobō, 1983).

3. Bandō Mariko, *Nihon no josei dētābanku* [*Data Bank of Japanese Women*] (Printing Office, Finance Ministry, 1992), 27.

4. To put these changes in proper perspective, however, I should note that many women in Japan still adhere to traditional roles as homemakers. Various studies show that Japanese women overwhelmingly support a clear division of labor by gender—a notion that fosters a pattern in which women between the ages of twenty-five and thirty-four (the prime child-rearing years) quit their jobs in large numbers.

5. According to a 1984 Ministry of Labor study, as many as 64 percent of businesses and industries had a policy of not interviewing new female college graduates at all that year. One cannot, however, totally deny the employers' common view that new female recruits tend to see employment as a chance to "participate in the real world" and to find a future husband; many, therefore, choose large, well-known firms. Living with their parents, many of these young women spend their money on themselves (financing their hobbies and leisure activities) as well as save for their weddings. According to sociologist Hara Kimi, however, it is the low status assigned to women in the workplace that makes women with four-year college educations quit. Hara has also maintained that employers in fact prefer two-year college graduates not only because they can be hired for less but also because they are in fact more ready to quit at marriage, thus encouraging the circulation of cheaper labor. Joseigaku kenkyū kai, "Onnatachi no ima" ["Women's Reality Today"], *Kōza Joseigaku* [*Lectures on Women's Studies*], vol. 2 (Keisō shobō, 1984), 67.

6. In the post-Equal Employment Opportunity Law era, the situation has improved even further; in 1989, a Ministry of Labor study showed that women held 5 percent of *kakarichō* positions and 2.1 percent of *kachō* (department head) positions.

7. One medical researcher felt that she had been prevented from studying a more serious topic during her training because she was a woman. Others expressed frustration at the difficulty of reaching higher, more responsible positions during internships and residencies. *Asahi Shimbun* (18 March 1984).

8. *Kōbe Shimbun* (7 December 1984).

9. The two-year college in Japan represents a completely separate educational track, without the possibility of transferring to a four-year institution. Furthermore, many of the graduates of two-year colleges major in such traditionally female fields as nursing, home economics, and preschool education.

10. There has been virtually no change over the past thirty years in the number of women who major in the fields of the humanities and natural sciences (around 35 and 2 percent, respectively), although the numbers of those studying education has declined considerably. According to the 1986 census, women made up just 6.4 percent of scientists, 2.4 percent of engineers, and 9.3 percent of lawyers.

11. According to a 1991 Ministry of Construction study, more than half of all construction businesses either have already employed or are going to employ women as engineers. *Look Japan* (December 1992). This figure, however, represents only 4 percent of all companies in Japan.

12. *Look Japan* (August 1989).

13. *Asahi Jānaru* (30 June 1989).

14. *Asahi Jānaru* (30 March 1984).

15. Sakamoto Fukuko, *Josei no kenri* [*Women's Rights*] (Hōritsu bunka sha, 1982), 241.

16. *Japan Times* (7 June 1991).

17. *Japan Times* (9 July 1992).

18. According to the Tokyo metropolitan government, however, only 10 percent of its 1,600 day-care centers were open longer in 1992.

19. *Asahi Jānaru* (30 June 1989).

20. While almost all companies have started to offer this opportunity (although less than 1 percent with full salary and 70 percent with partial pay), nearly six months after the introduction of the law, two-thirds of the companies reportedly had no applicants. *Japan Times* (31 March 1993).

21. Most part-timers are paid hourly wages, the average of which was 712 yen ($5.90) in 1990. Even though part-timers who have been working for several years in one job are not uncommon nowadays, most part-timers receive no lump-sum retirement money.

22. In 1973, when the Japanese economy slowed down, the number of workers, both men and women, was reduced; when the economy recovered, women were hired back as part-timers. The Japanese economy went through another slowdown in 1979, but this time it was only part-time women who were fired. "Onnatachi no ima," ["Women's Reality Today"], *Kōza Joseigaku* [*Lectures on Women's Studies*], vol. 2 (Keisō shobō, 1984).

23. A 1989 study by Nihon Rōdōkenkyū kikō [Japan Labor Research Organization] showed that 14 percent of respondents stated that they were part-timers because full-time jobs were not available. Bandō, 57.

24. *Japan Times* (14 April 1993).

25. A third type of working arrangement, referred to as *naishoku*, or "in-the-house work," is for those unwilling to leave home for various reasons and who therefore bring work to their houses. Although decreasing in number in recent years, such workers worked hours as long as part-timers but earned less; they supported Japan's economic boom during the 1960s and 1970s. One woman, for instance, having moved to a newly developed suburb at the end of 1979, needed extra income to cover the mortgage, as well as the increasing cost of education and food. She was attracted to the idea of making 1,500 yen ($12) a day stuffing envelopes. The work was time consuming, requiring help from her husband and mother-in-law to meet deadlines. For many years after the end of World War II and before part-time employment became popular, *naishoku* had been a common way for Japanese wives to make small amounts of money on their own. The work they do is subcontracted by factories and firms (which are often subcontractors themselves), some manufacturing toys and parts of electric appliances. The average pay for this type of job was as low as 289 yen ($1.25) an hour in the early 1980s. Women who engage in *naishoku* tend to be older than those who go out to work. Some newcomers in this category, particularly women with skills they can perform at home, such as word-processing and software development, can, however, command considerably higher wages. Nearly 1 million women are now estimated to be working in this type of arrangement.

26. *Japan Times* (30 June 1991).

27. *Japan Times* (25 May 1993).

28. Prime Minister's Office, Labor Force Survey, 1979, in *Hachijūnendai no josei no seikatsu*, 58.

CHAPTER 7

1. With the decline in the birth rate, many Japanese are growing up as only children. According to my friends in Japan, some such young people seem to be delaying marriage or staying single altogether. Both my brother, virtually an only child (since I live outside Japan), and my cousin might fall in this group of people. Both my mother and aunt became widows during their forties, but, being influenced by the traditional Confucian doctrine of not having "more than one master," they, like many other women of their generation, did not remarry. This sort of situation sometimes makes it difficult for children to leave their single parents to get married and set up households. Also, since many young women in Japan are reluctant to live in a non-nuclear family household, marriage between an only son and an only daughter is extremely difficult.

2. *Asahi Shimbun* (18 March 1984).

3. In a 1986 Management and Coordination Agency survey, only 25 percent of the respondents said that they would "do all they could" to care for their parents. This was the second lowest response after Sweden, and about half that of American counterparts. *Look Japan* (January 1993).

4. *Look Japan* (January 1993). The technological revolution and rapid urbanization of the late 1950s and 1960s have affected the lives of all Japanese, but particularly those of the elderly. The difficulty of fitting into the new lifestyle and environment is no doubt at least partly behind the high suicide rate among elderly Japanese.

5. *Fujin Kōron* (November 1982).

6. *Asahi Shimbun* (10 December 1990).

7. Employers can now provide up to three months of unpaid (or partially paid) leave for both men and women to care for elderly parents and parents-in-law (as well as sick children and spouses).

8. The need for such facilities is not small, as often shown by long waiting lists. According to a Ministry of Welfare study, only 4 percent of these residents receive visitors more frequently than twice a week; about 30 percent have no visitors at all.

9. As of 1993, the average cost of these facilities, generally referred to as *yūryō rōjin hōmu*, or elderly people's homes for fees, was a 30 million yen ($226,000) entry fee, in addition to a monthly charge of about 144,000 yen ($1,320) for room and board. There are 261 such privately run facilities throughout Japan, caring for 19,000 elderlies. The media have reported recently that, despite their luxurious looks, the care in these profit-driven facilities is less than desirable.

CHAPTER 8

1. Unlike feminist movements in the United States, however, publicly declared lesbianism did not develop as an important aspect of sexual liberation in Japan. Only a few small groups, such as one that started a magazine called *Onna: Erosu* [*Women: Eros*], discussed and practiced bisexualism and lesbianism.

2. Tsunoda Yukiko, *Kawaru josei no sekai* [*A Changing World of Women*] (Rōdō kyōiku sentā, 1986), 326.

3. Inoue Teruko, *Joseigaku to sono shūhen* [*Women's Studies and Other Issues*] (Keiso shobo, 1980), 225.

4. Tanaka Mitsu, *Kono michi hito suji* [*Only This Path*] (Ribu Wuman Senta, 1972).

5. *Agora*, 104 (December 1980).

6. Ibid., 66.

7. *Asahi Shimbun* (5 October 1993).

8. *Asahi Jānaru* (17 November 1989).

9. *Japan Times* (25 March 1993).

10. Ehara Yumiko, a feminist scholar, has stated that the Japanese media's response to sexual harassment was by far quicker—because it is about sex—than their response to other women's issues, such as wage discrimination. *Asahi Jānaru* (17 November 1989).

11. A 1990 Ministry of Labor survey found that nearly half (42 percent) of women managers reported that they had experienced some form of sexual harassment. *Yomiuri Shimbun* (21 January 1991).

12. Many companies have annual team-building retreats, often at hot springs. New female recruits on one company tour were harassed by older company men who would peek into the women's section of the public baths, in accordance with an unwritten company tradition. Because of this "traditional" practice, these men were unable to view their actions as sexual harassment.

13. Ōshima Shizuko and Carolyn Francis, *HELP kara mita Nihon* [*Japan Seen from HELP*]. (Asahi Shimbun sha, 1988), 263–65.

14. The textbooks used in Japanese public schools are centrally monitored by the national government and need the approval of the Ministry of Education prior to classroom usage. According to a survey, the gender imbalance among the judges who evaluated and approved the textbooks was apparent; likewise, authors of textbooks were heavily biased by gender: eight women in contrast to 714 men. *Bessatsu Takarajima 4: Onna no Jiten* [*Women's Dictionary*] (JICC Publisher, 1977).

CHAPTER 9

1. *Asahi Jānaru* (4 August 1989).
2. Criticism of Mr. Uno's conduct by various women's groups such as *Shufuren*, the National Housewives Association, was, however, quite severe; women who saw a basic sexist attitude behind his remarks about his "paid mistress" felt that there was a connection to a prevailing double standard, manifested in Japanese businessmen's sex tours to Southeast Asian countries as well as in the "importing" of Asian female workers for prostitution.
3. The Japanese Diet consists of two houses: the Upper House of Councilors (252 seats) and the Lower House of Representatives (512 seats). The function of the upper house, where a proportional representation system is partially used, is considered mainly to be a check against the excessive power of the lower house; most ministers are chosen from the House of Representatives, and it is here that chances of gaining access to the inner circles of power exist.
4. In an international comparison, done by IPU in June 1993, Japan ranked 128th out of 156 nations throughout the world in female representation in the lower house; *Asahi Shimbun* (23 October 1993). In April 1994, a woman Supreme Court judge was appointed by the Hosokawa administration for the first time in Japan's judicial history; as for judges in general, there has been some increase in the percentage of women (from 2.1 percent in 1977 to 5 percent in 1990). The number of women appointed to various national-level councils has increased nearly fourfold in the past fifteen years but remains relatively miniscule at only 8.2 percent of all positions.
5. Her casual mannerisms, her clear and unpretentious way of speaking, and her tall and sturdy (rather than delicate and feminine) stature are also said to be sources of her popularity among women voters.
6. Madonna does not refer to the American singer. Although the term's origin is not clear, it probably derives from the nickname of a popular Japanese television character, a woman with considerable charm and integrity.
7. Women candidates who were persuaded by Doi to run for election have been inexperienced in politics and sometime ambivalent about their roles. Doi's ability to inspire these women, however, has not been small. Once they entered the political arena, many seemed to have gained confidence and put their leadership skills to work.

8. Even earlier, in 1977, a women's group was organized in Kyoto in support of Yoshitake Teruko, who ran for an Upper House seat. Yoshitake lost the election that time, but the group continued and moved on to other causes, such as demanding child-care space in city office buildings frequently used by women.

9. The number of women elected to local legislatures has also increased, slowly but steadily, over the years: 1 percent in 1976 to 2.2 percent in 1987. Since the conservative LDP paid them little attention, women were attracted to the JSP, particularly because of Doi's leadership. The LDP's strategy for attracting women voters, particularly in national elections, has been to use the personal popularity of their candidates, such as former Olympic medalists, actresses, and so forth. Considering women to be unequipped with "political instincts," senior party members have refused to see women as partners who can voice their own opinions and form their own policies.

10. The person in this position, for instance, receives weekly briefings from the Vice-Minister for Foreign Affairs and the director of the Cabinet Information Research Office, the Japanese version of the Central Intelligence Agency (CIA) in the United States.

11. Both Takahara and Moriyama stayed in their respective positions for only six months. The Kaifu cabinet was reshuffled after only ten months; although Miyazawa appointed Santō Akiko (a former actress) as head of the Science and Technology Agency, his administration had no woman at a similar level or position.

12. Doi was also sometimes criticized for her ignorance of basic political knowledge, her unwillingness to engage in behind-the-scenes dealings, and her inflexible opposition on principle, as seen during the Persian Gulf crisis, when she opposed Japanese participation in the United Nations peace-keeping organization.

13. "The Socialist party is a man's party ... until a better person appeared, we were putting on a show," according to a chief party member quoted in *Asahi Shimbun* (28 July 1990).

14. The traditional Japanese high regard for civil servants and trust that the bureaucracy, rather than the legislature, will run the country may well be a factor behind this reluctance to take political policies seriously as a way to enhance women's status.

15. With fourteen new seats added, women now occupy 6.8 percent of the 763 seats of the Diet.

Selected Bibliography

Bernstein, Gail Lee. *Haruko's World: A Japanese Farm Woman and Her Community.* Stanford, CA: Stanford University Press, 1983.

———, ed. *Recreating Japanese Women, 1600–1945.* Berkeley: University of California Press, 1991.

Bingham, Marjorie Wall, and Susan Gross. *Women in Japan from Ancient Times to the Present.* St. Louis Park, Minnesota: Glenhurst Publications, 1987.

Christopher, Robert C. *The Japanese Mind.* New York: Linden Press, 1983.

Cordon, Jane. *A Half Step Behind: Japanese Women of the 80s.* New York: Dodd, Mead, 1985.

Dalby, Liza. *Geisha.* Tokyo: Kodansha International, 1983.

Davidson, Cathy N. *36 Views of Mount Fuji: On Finding Myself in Japan.* New York: Dutton, 1993.

Halloran, Richard. *Japan: Images and Realities.* Tokyo: Charles E. Tuttle, 1969.

Hane Mikiso, tr. and ed. *Reflections on the Way to the Gallows: Voices of Japanese Rebel Women.* New York: Pantheon Books and University of California Press, 1988.

Imamura, Anne. *Urban Japanese Housewives.* Honolulu: University of Hawaii Press, 1987.

Ishimoto Shizue. *Facing Two Ways: The Story of My Life.* Stanford, CA: Stanford University Press, 1984.

Iwao Sumiko. *The Japanese Woman: Traditional Images & Changing Reality.* New York: Free Press, 1993.

Kittridge, Cherry. *Womansword: What Japanese Words Say About Women.* Tokyo, New York: Kōdansha International, 1987.

Kiyoka Eiichi, tr. and ed. *Fukuzawa Yukichi on Japanese Women.* Tokyo: Tokyo University Press, 1983.

Kuroyanagi Tetsuko. *Totto-chan, the Little Girl at the Window.* Trans. Dorothy Britton. Tokyo: Kōdansha International, 1982.

Lebra, Joyce, Joy Paulson, and Elizabeth Powers, eds. *Women in Changing Japan.* Stanford, CA: Stanford University Press, 1976.

Lebra, Takie Sugiyama. *Japanese Women: Constraints and Fulfillment.* Honolulu: University of Hawaii Press, 1984.

Pharr, Susan J. *Political Women in Japan: The Search for a Place in Political Life.* Berkeley: University of California Press, 1981.

Rauch, Jonathan. *The Outnation.* Boston: Harvard Business School Press, 1992.

Robbins-Mowry, Dorothy. *The Hidden Sun: Women of Modern Japan.* Boulder, CO: Westview Press, 1983.

Sievers, Sharon. *Flowers in Salt: The Beginnings of Feminist Consciousness in Modern Japan.* Stanford, CA: Stanford University Press, 1983.

Smith, Robert J., and Ella Lury Wiswell. *The Women of Suye Mura.* Chicago: University of Chicago Press, 1982.

Sugano Kimiko. *Kimiko's World.* San Francisco: Strawberry Hill Press, 1982.

Tanaka Kazuko. *A Short History of the Women's Movement in Modern Japan.* Tokyo: Femintern Press, 1974.

Trager, James. *Letters from Sachiko: A Japanese Woman's View of Life in the Land of the Economic Miracle.* New York: Atheneum, 1982.

Tsurumi Kazuko. *Social Change and the Individual: Japan Before and After Defeat in World War II.* Princeton, NJ: Princeton University Press, 1970.

Vogel, Ezra F. *Japan's New Middle Class: The Salary Man and His Family in a Tokyo Suburb.* Berkeley: University of California Press, 1971.

SUGGESTED FICTION

Ariyoshi Sawako. *The Doctor's Wife.* Tokyo: Kōdansha International, 1978.

——. *The Twilight Years.* Trans. Mildred Tahara. Tokyo: Kōdansha International, 1984.

Enchi Fumiko. *The Waiting Years.* Tokyo: Kōdansha International, 1971.

Mizuta Lippit, Noriko, and Kyoko Iriye Selden, tr. and ed. *Japanese Women Writers: Twentieth Century Short Fiction.* Armonk, NY: M. E. Sharpe, 1991.

Tanaka Yukiko, ed. *To Live and to Write: Selections by Japanese Women Writers 1913–1938.* Seattle, WA: Seal Press, 1987.

————, tr. and ed. *Unmapped Territories: New Women's Fiction from Japan.* Seattle, WA: Women In Translation, 1991.

Tanaka Yukiko, and Elizabeth Hanson, ed. *This Kind of Woman: Ten Stories by Japanese Women Writers, 1960–1976.* New York: Perigee Books, 1982.

Ueda Makoto, ed. *The Mother of Dreams and Other Short Stories: Portrayals of Women in Modern Japanese Fiction.* Tokyo: Kōdansha International, 1989.

Index

Management, 104, 107–8, 112, 113; position, 107; promotion into, 109; skill, 162; women managers, 109, 122
Manpower Dispatching Business Law, 121
Marriage agency, 16, 17, 167 n.9; go-between, 32; matchmaking, 17
Motherhood, 59, 64, 116
Mother-in-law, 127, 137
Miai, 11–16, 29, 32, 77, 166 n.4
Minikomi, 123
Mitchie Boom, 13
Moriyama Mayumi, 159
Mura, David, 14

Naishoku (in-the-house work), 176 n.26
Narayamabushi kō (by Fukazawa Shichiro), 149
Narita divorce, 49
National Council of Women's Organization of Agricultural Cooperatives, 153; Federation of Regional Women's Organizations, 153; Health Insurance, 136–37; Housewives Association, 179
Network of women, 124, 150–51; networking, 108; the Network Sisters, 149
News media, 141, 144, 147, 149–50, 158; Western, 1, 39, 66
Nuclear disarmament, 151
Nuclear family, 3, 14, 59, 130, 166 n.3
Nursing home, 137–39
Nyū taun (new town), 61, 63

Old age, 134, 138–39, 154

Onna: Erosu (*Women: Eros*), 178 n.1
Onna kara onna tachi e (From a Woman to Women), 145
Onna no nettowākingu (*Women's Networking*), 150–51, 153
Otsuka Eiji, 81–82

Pachinko scandal, 160
Part-timers, 90, 103, 115–20, 148, 176 n.21; union, 120
Politics, 156, 159, 161–62; contribution, 160; involvement, 156; Japanese, 157; party, 160; political clout, 159; representation, 156; ties, 158
Pornography, 90, 92, 94–95
Postwar years, 4–6, 22–23, 59, 127
Procreation, 12
Promotion, 101, 103, 105, 107, 109, 112–13, 168 n.2
Prostitution, 90–92, 152, 173 n.24, 179 n.2; among teenage girls, 86–89
Protective measures (for women at work place), 113–14

Ranma 1/2, 83. *See also* Girls' comics
Rape, 174 n.31
Remarriage, 52
Ren'ai, 12–16, 81, 166 nn.2, 4; *kurabu* (club), 81
Rōjin hōmu, 139, 177 n.9. *See also* Nursing home
Role model, 149

Saitō Kiyomi, 107–8
Saitō Shigeo, 31, 133
Sarari (salaried) man, 18, 132

ABOUT THE AUTHOR

YUKIKO TANAKA is a professional writer and translator. She has published *This Kind of Woman: Ten Stories By Japanese Women Writers, 1960–1976* (1982); *To Live and To Write: Selections by Japanese Women Writers, 1913–1938* (1987); and *Unmapped Territories: New Women's Fiction from Japan* (1991).

ISBN 0-275-95067-0

90000>

EAN

9 780275 950675

HARDCOVER BAR CODE